The Right Food for Kids

The Right Food for Kids

A parents' guide to healthy eating for children

Louise Templeton

Photographs by
Anthea Sieveking

Foreword by
Dr A.J. Franklin
Consultant Paediatrician
St John's Hospital, Chelmsford

CENTURY PUBLISHING
LONDON

Also available from Century

The Breastfeeding Book Máire Messenger
Exercises for Childbirth Barbara Dale and Johanna Roeber
Postnatal Exercises Barbara Whiteford and Margie Polden
Toddler Taming Dr Christopher Green
Twins Averil Clegg and Anne Woollett

The Right Food for your Kids:
A parents' guide to healthy eating for children
was conceived, edited and designed by
Frances Lincoln Limited,
Apollo Works, 5 Charlton Kings Road, London NW5 2SB

Consultant dietician
Sue Lupson BSc, SRD

Filmsetting by D. P. Media Limited, Hitchin, Hertfordshire

First published in Great Britain in 1984
by Century Publishing Co. Ltd
First published as a paperback in 1985
by Century Publishing Co. Ltd,
Portland House,
12–13 Greek Street, London W1V 5LE

British Library Cataloguing in Publication Data

Templeton, Louise
The right food for your kids.
1. Children – Nutrition
I. Title
613.2′088054 RJ206

ISBN 0 7126 0940 7 (paper)
ISBN 0 7126 0498 7 (cased)

Printed and bound in Yugoslavia
by Mladinska knjiga, Ljubljana

Contents

Foreword

Why do we need another book on how to feed children? The last twenty-five years has seen a revolution in the eating patterns of our society with the introduction of a dazzling array of new processed foods readily available and needing very little preparation. For busy people this has meant a great saving of time and effort and the food processing industry has made great efforts to make this food attractive even to quite small children.

But this change to convenient foods, available all year round, has blinded us to the content of our diet – is it adequate, not just in calories for energy but in the essential nutrients our bodies need for health? And for children whose metabolism is geared for growth, this balance of the right materials must be even more important.

Sadly we must admit that the evidence of sub-optimal nutrition is growing steadily and despite the fact that the late Adelle Davis pointed this out over thirty years ago to the American public, the message has not been accepted here, either by the medical profession or the fast food manufacturers.

Louise Templeton has produced a timely reminder to modern mums of the basic principles of good nutrition and a wealth of detailed information about the values, advantages and disadvantages of common foods. Her very strong emphasis on basic foodstuffs is a welcome antidote to the skilled and clamorous advertising of the food processing industry. It may come as a shock to some mothers to discover that babies and young children can be fed from available fresh foods and cereals rather than from the much publicized baby foods in tins, jars and packets found on the shelves of the local pharmacy. Even the suggestion that babies should be weaned off milk feeds by the age of 1 year (following the pattern of all other mammals) may raise a few eyebrows, but as cow's milk is at the top of everyone's list of foods that cause problems – this is good sense.

Starting from before the child is even conceived, the author provides detailed advice for each stage – pre-conception, early and late pregnancy, and through the first two years of the infant's life and beyond. The importance of pre-conception preparation is only just being recognized but the discovery that some neural tube malformations could be prevented by the addition of vitamins of the B group to the parents' diet before conception focused attention on the possibility that foetal development and the health of the child before its birth may be influenced by the chemical environment in which it is conceived and developed. We know that smoking even in very early pregnancy can affect the number of respiratory infections a child may develop in his or her first year of life and that infantile colic and eczema may be influenced by the mother's diet when breastfeeding. So if we are planning to have only one or two children, it seems pertinent to conceive them when we are at the peak of physical well-being.

As a paediatrician I find I need dietetic advice frequently for the parents of my young patients and I welcome this book for its simple and forthright message. I hope it will also find its way into the hands of every health visitor, midwife and nursery nurse and also those who buy the food for school kitchens. So many kids seem to suffer from recurrent infections and glue ear, allergic reactions of all kinds, bowel disorders and hyperactive overstimulation from food additives that anything that helps to prevent these disorders must be welcome. And the specific needs of the young diabetic, coeliac or obese patients have not been forgotten either.

To the parents who care about these things I commend this small book which is packed with goodness and sound nutritional wisdom. Naturally we are concerned about today's killing diseases, cardiovascular degeneration and cancers of all kinds; we should note the suggestion that the foundations of many of these diseases are laid by the dietary habits of childhood. But a word of encouragement to those giving the extra time and effort needed to prepare the healthier diet, the reward will be healthier children and not only so, but a rediscovery of the excitement of good cooking and the satisfaction of knowing that you are laying a good foundation as you see your child develop a robust appetite.

Alan Franklin, FRCP, DCH, DRCOG,
Consultant Paediatrician
St John's Hospital, Chelmsford

1 The right food for your family

Food is vital to health

Increasing research shows nutrition to be the single most important factor in determining the state of our health. Today alarming numbers of adults and children too are found to be suffering from a wide range of serious degenerative diseases such as cardiovascular degeneration and cancers of all kinds. Many of these conditions have now been clearly linked with inadequate diets containing a surfeit of highly processed and refined foods, high in fat, sugar and salt and other additives, and all too low in fresh fruit, vegetables and grains. The effects of bad diet can no longer be ignored.

But the care we take in ensuring our children have a healthy diet must begin with the care we take in eating well ourselves. Like all other aspects of behaviour, children learn good or bad eating habits from the example set by their parents.

Parental diet and the unborn child

A child's health is, to a great extent, determined many months before his or her conception, it is now agreed by many eminent researchers and scientists in the field of human medicine. It has long been acknowledged that good ante-natal care is very important in helping to ensure women have successful pregnancies and births but it is now being increasingly recognized that the pre-conceptual health of both parents is also an important factor in determining the future health of a baby.

A child's constitution, its inborn strengths and weaknesses, is the result of specific factors (known scientifically as genes) which are passed on from generation to generation in the sperm and ovum produced by the child's father and mother. The father's contribution to this process is equally as important as the mother's – a factor which has always been recognized in breeding prize bulls and stallions! The quality of the genetic material passed on to the next generation in the sperm is greatly determined by the health and nutritional status of the father so that whether he smokes or drinks or has a bad diet will affect more than his own health. Similarly, the mother's health before, during and after pregnancy will also greatly affect not only her own physical and mental well-being but that of her child. Therefore, both parents should take steps to improve their overall health before conception of the planned child.

The right food is vital for the health of all the family, including the unborn baby

Even today it is not widely realized that certain inherited characteristics can be altered by dietary practice. In the 1940s, a dentist called Weston A. Price from Cleveland, Ohio, visited fourteen 'primitive' races in their native habitats. His original intention was to investigate the effects of environment and lifestyle upon tooth decay but he made another fascinating discovery. When the parents changed from eating locally grown produce to eating imported, refined foods the health of the children born following the dietary change was inferior to those born before. Not only did the children's teeth suffer but also specific facial changes were noted, such as a narrowing of the skull resulting in distorted vision; breathing difficulties; overcrowding of teeth and, in some cases, reduced mental capacity and brain damage. Similar observations have been made elsewhere, amongst the youngest children of large, poor families. Yet it was of great significance that in all the cases studied, children were no longer born with deformed facial structure when their parents reverted to their native diet based on fresh, local produce of animal and vegetable origin.

Foetal development

During the first weeks of pregnancy the foetus develops with amazing rapidity. By the end of the fourth week after conception the entire backbone and spine are established, by the seventh week the face is completely formed and by the end of the third month the legs can kick and the fingers grasp. All this takes place before many women realize they are pregnant and the foetus can be severely affected by poor diet during this period. Therefore, it is crucial that women have a good, preconceptual eating pattern to ensure the health of their babies.

There are many healthy people and communities to be found throughout the world living on a variety of different diets but they all tend to have one important factor in common. They base their food choice on locally grown, seasonal produce and much of it is eaten raw or subjected to only a little processing to make it palatable and digestible. Yet in communities where large quantities of refined and processed foods are eaten, such as our own, numerous health problems have arisen. This is partly because eating habits have changed drastically, particularly in the west, over the last century with the advent of chemical fertilizers, and intensive, factory farming methods and processes which refine the nourishment out of food.

The problem with convenience foods

There are relatively few prospective parents today who are eating the same diet as their grandparents. Microwave ovens, deep freezers and convenience foods are all comparatively recent innovations and although in most countries of the world, certain traditional dishes are still in use, call into a supermarket in Europe, Scandinavia or North America and familiar products will be visible on every shelf: soft drinks, instant pizzas, hamburgers, potato crisps, tins and packets which all promise convenience for the user and excitement for the tastebuds. Look at the ingredients on the labels and repeatedly the same items occur such as antioxidants and monosodium glutamate. Try deleting from your shopping list all foods containing sugar, salt, refined wheat and maize (corn), artificial colourings, flavourings and preservatives. This, you will find, eliminates about 80 per cent of your groceries. What is left are the foods that have supported human life throughout the ages, such as fresh and dried fruits and vegetables, wholegrain cereals, pulses, nuts, seeds and fresh fish. Sadly, eggs, dairy produce and meats are rarely additive-free.

What should we eat?

So, what should we eat to ensure a healthy, well-balanced diet both for ourselves and our children?

Although growing children have higher and more specific nutrient needs than adults during the first 7 years of life, basically, what is good food for children is good food for adults too. If parents are erratic eaters it will be difficult for them to ensure that their children have healthy eating habits as these are mainly learned in the home during the early years.

Avoid refined foods

A well-balanced diet is based on fresh wholefoods. Fresh meaning the best quality seasonal or dried produce; whole, meaning as complete in structure and nutrient composition as possible, in order to include in the diet all known and as yet unknown factors, required for sound health. To ensure healthy growth in a child all essential food factors are required as even temporary deficiencies can have long-term repercussions. All highly refined and processed foods and those containing additives or preservatives should be avoided as the original nutrient balance, so essential for good health, is upset during refining and processing. Even a refined product fortified with a selection of the nutrients lost in refining, is still only a partial food. However, a certain amount of processing is required to make some foods safe or digestible. Cooking is the most basic form of home processing and when properly carried out can enhance nutrient absorption and utilization, but some nutrients will inevitably be lost as a result of heat sensitivity and solubility.

Should we be vegetarian?

Controversy still exists over whether the human body was designed for the consumption of plant or animal foods. The true carnivores, members of the cat family, still require some plant foods for balanced nutrition. This they find in the form of wild herbs in the stomachs of their kill. No carnivore feeds upon lean meat entirely. A study of the diets throughout the world soon reveals the adaptability of the human body to widely differing environments and foods. But one common factor is the existence of a staple in the diet, in other words, a food around which the diet is based and in most cases this is a cereal grain.

A varied diet is best

Generally speaking, the more varied the supply of foods, animal and plant, the less likelihood there is of dietary deficiencies. Animal foods are not essential in a diet adequate in plant foods supplying all the essential nutrients. However, there are no diets where plant food is not included. Even Eskimos, generally regarded as exclusive meat- and fish-eaters, also make use of berries, herbs and roots in season. The structure of human teeth and the digestive tract suggest that humans are omniverous (able to feed on all kinds of food) but with a distinct need for a diet based on high fibre plant foods.

Those who do not eat meat can consult Appendix 2 (see page 117) for an explanation of protein complementation and suggestions for combining foods to make complete proteins.

How to ensure a healthy diet

So now, the questions that spring to the mind of every new or prospective parent are – What foods? How much? How often?

There should be no doubt in anyone's mind that the ideal first food for babies is mother's milk (see section on breastfeeding in Chapter 2). Knowing what constitutes a healthy, nutritionally well-balanced diet will safeguard the mother's health while breastfeeding when her appetite will be greatly increased, otherwise the baby's nutrient needs could be met at the expense of the mother's who would have to provide these from her own body stores.

Seasonal foods

Eating seasonally gives the widest possible choice of fresh foods, appropriate for the time of year. This makes sense physiologically and financially. Hot, dry days reduce the appetite making seasonal and readily available fresh fruits and vegetables the natural choice for snacks and meals. In winter, it is foolish to buy expensive, limp, tasteless, hothouse lettuce and tomatoes when fresh root vegetables (carrots, parsnips, turnips, beetroots) and leafy greens (Brussels sprouts, broccoli, cabbage) can be used raw or lightly steamed in soups and casseroles at a much lower cost. Cooked meals with bean and seed sprouts and lacto-fermented (non-vinegar) pickles are generally more appealing on cold, damp days and more appropriate at this time of year than summer salads.

Wholefoods can look good

Nourishing food should also look, taste and smell appealing. Few commercially processed foods can claim to be genuinely nutritious yet highly nutritious health foods often lack the eye appeal at which supermarket packaging excels. Unappetizing meals can be as much the fault of the cook as the food itself. With proper handling and presentation the majority of wholefoods can rival the most cleverly contrived TV dinner. A glance through an Oriental cookery book reveals how a skilful use of contrasting colour, texture and flavour, results in satisfying and attractive dishes. It is this high standard of cooking and presentation which will probably be required to sell the idea of healthy eating to your family, for it is essential to re-educate the whole family's attitude if good habits are to be inherited by the new generation (for information about cooking techniques and food preparation see Appendix 3 page 118).

However, it is often at the onset of pregnancy that many women, and increasingly men, begin to show more interest in their living habits. Yet it is important not to be off-putting. Eating for health is sometimes associated with crankiness rather than plain commonsense. Every parent must avoid that universally unpopular command, 'Eat it up! It's good for you.'

Only eat when you are hungry

One of the problems in the affluent west is our tendency to overeat. Good nutrition is as much about what and when *not* to eat as it is about the kinds of food to include in a healthy diet. However, good habits are easier to give up than bad ones and this was never more true than when talking about eating. Surveys on obesity show that many overweight people do not eat more food than thin people but they eat whether or not they are hungry – more out of habit than actual need. The use of food as an emotional prop could well be a throw-back to childhood when a favourite food was given as a consolation for disappointment. Similarly, commands to 'Clean up your plate!' have created guilt feelings in some people about 'wasting' leftover food. The result is that many mothers become human waste-disposal units consuming the remnants of their child's meal in addition to their own.

Know your nutrients

Confusing as it all may seem at first glance there are some definite guidelines which can be followed and an explanation of the nutrients and where they can be found is a help in choosing food. The nutrients we need include protein, fat, carbohydrate, vitamins, minerals and trace elements and these are most readily found in fresh wholefoods grown in healthy soil. No one food supplies all nutrients and most foods supply more than one. To achieve a balanced diet a selection of foods is required.

The importance of nutrients

Insufficient research has so far been completed to provide detailed charts of food sources of all known nutrients, let alone those nutrients yet to be discovered. The following chart is given as a guide to outline the nutrient content of a variety of foods with a brief indication of the nutrient's function. It is sufficient to realize that if a food component has achieved the status of becoming a nutrient, it is essential for maintaining the healthy function of the human body. Furthermore, the wholesomeness of a food goes beyond its nutrient content. Evidence suggests that food grown in nutrient-rich soil by bio-dynamic/organic methods (grown without the use of artificial fertilizers, herbicides or pesticides) is higher in nutrient content than commercially grown produce and free from traces of potentially harmful chemical residues. Therefore the inclusion of bio-dynamically/organically grown raw food in the diet is particularly important in supplying those nutrients destroyed by heat and processing.

Protein

Protein is concerned with the growth and repair of damaged cells and can be found in both animal and vegetable foods. Because it is concerned with general body maintenance, protein is often referred to as the building blocks of the body and although much emphasis is put on the need for protein, no one nutrient is more important than another for good health.

There are many hundreds of proteins in the body. These are made up of varying combinations of simpler substances known as amino acids of which there are over twenty. Eight of these (ten for children) are called 'essential amino acids' as they cannot be produced in the body but must be provided in the diet. All the essential amino acids are contained in animal proteins. Vegetable proteins (other than soya beans) lack or are low in one or more of the essentials. So animal protein is known as *complete protein* and vegetable protein as *incomplete protein*.

By combining plant foods however, the absence or deficiency of one amino acid can be complemented by its excess in another plant food to make a complete protein. (For examples of complementation see Appendix 2 page 117). Eaten in excess of needs, protein is used as an energy source or stored as fat which is wasteful. Expensive, high-protein slimming diets are potentially harmful as they can overstress the body.

Carbohydrates

Carbohydrates are good energy sources and comprise the starches and the sugars. The most useful sources are those which also contain dietary fibre, essential for the proper function of the digestive tract. All starches and most sugars are broken down by digestion into glucose which is the main fuel of the body. Certain vitamins, minerals and enzymes are required for the proper use of carbohydrates. If these are absent, as in refined white sugar and white flour, the body has to acquire these nutrients from another source. If body stores are called upon too frequently they will become depleted and could result in a breakdown of health. Only the wholefood carbohydrates listed under starches supply the necessary co-nutrients.

Fibre

Natural fibre or cellulose is found in plant foods and because of its indigestibility it was, for many years, regarded as unnecessary and potentially harmful. Although not a nutrient, fibre is now recognized as a dietary essential for the health of the digestive tract. Lack of fibre results in constipation and associated diseases which include diverticulitis and colon cancer.

Fat

Fats (saturated, unsaturated and polyunsaturated) are an alternative energy source supplying twice the energy as the same amount of carbohydrate or protein. Some fats also contain the fat-soluble vitamins A, D, E and K. A certain amount of fat in the body is important for the protection and insulation of vital organs. Cholesterol is an important constituent of the blood, involved in supplying energy to the muscles and laying down fat stores. There is no need for dietary cholesterol as adequate supplies are produced in the body. Cholesterol in the diet comes only from foods of animal origin. Too much saturated fat in the diet alters the blood composition and raises the cholesterol level which is linked with heart, blood, and artery disorders. Polyunsaturated fatty acids are essential for cell structure. Soft margarines made from vegetable and seed oils claim certain health benefits but butter is still a more natural product. Too much of any type of fat results in overweight and scientific research suggests using fat in moderation.

Vitamins, minerals and trace elements

Essential for the proper function of the body, these are required in varying amounts from a trace to hundreds of milligrams a day and their absence soon results in disease. Some can be stored in the body (fat-soluble vitamins) but most have to be supplied by the daily food intake. The absorption of certain vitamins and minerals is often assisted by the presence of another nutrient, for example vitamin C aids iron absorption. Conversely, the excessive intake of one nutrient may inhibit the uptake or utilization of another as happens with copper and zinc. The taking of arbitrary amounts of randomly selected nutrient supplements can therefore be more harmful than helpful. For long-term as well as short-term benefit the most complete nourishment is best supplied by fresh wholefoods.

THE SOURCE AND FUNCTION OF NUTRIENTS

NUTRIENT	SOURCES	FUNCTION
Protein	*Animal proteins:* meat, poultry, fish, shellfish, eggs, milk, yoghurt, cheese. *Vegetable proteins:* pulses, soya flour, nuts, seeds, wholegrain cereals and breads, wheatgerm	Essential for growth, the repair of body cells, reproduction, blood formation, bone development, protection against infection
Carbohydrate	*Starch sources:* wholegrain cereals, wholemeal flours and breads, pulses, soya flour, potatoes *Sugar sources:* fresh and dried fruits, root vegetables, honey, grain syrups, maple syrup, unrefined sugar	Supplies energy which spares protein for its many other essential functions
Fibre	Wholegrain cereals, pulses, soya flour, nuts, seeds, dried and fresh fruits, vegetables	Necessary for the proper function of the digestive tract but it must be used with care in infant diets
Fat	*Cholesterol:* offal, meats, shellfish, egg yolk, butter, cheese *Saturated fat:* butter, cream, whole milk, cheeses, egg yolk, hard fats, animal fats, some margarines *Unsaturated and polyunsaturated fat:* fish oils, nuts and seeds (except avocado pears, cashew nuts and coconut which contain saturated fat), oils from nuts, seeds and grains, soft margarines	Essential for membranes, hormones and bile acids. A useful source of energy. Polyunsaturated fats help the absorption of vitamins A, D and E, help lower the blood cholesterol level and promote healthy skin and tissue cell structure. Too much fat of any kind contributes to excess weight
Fat-soluble vitamins **Vitamin A**	Oily fish, fish liver oils, liver, egg yolk, dairy produce, fortified margarine Carotene is converted to vitamin A in the body and is supplied by carrots, tomatoes, all green and some yellow vegetables, dried apricots, parsley, pumpkin, squash, swede, peas, prunes	Essential for proper function of eyesight. Important for normal growth and health of skin, hair and nails. Increases resistance to infection
Vitamin D	Oily fish, fish liver oils, egg yolk, dairy fats, fortified margarine, seaweeds (contain ergosterol one of the main components of usable vitamin D)	Formed in the body by the action of direct sunlight on the skin and essential for absorption of calcium required for bones and teeth. Absence can result in rickets
Vitamin E	Wheat, rice and oatgerms, wholegrain cereals, green leafy vegetables, nuts, seeds, pulses, soya flour, cold pressed vegetable oils	Improves general vitality. Important for integrity of cell structure and function of heart and muscles

THE SOURCE AND FUNCTION OF NUTRIENTS

NUTRIENT	SOURCES	FUNCTION
Vitamin K	Green leafy vegetables, tomatoes, liver, egg yolk, soya bean oil, seaweeds, alfalfa	Essential for blood clotting to prevent excess blood loss after injury
Water-soluble vitamins **B Group** **B1 Thiamin**	Wholegrain cereals especially cereal germs, brewer's yeast, yeast extracts, sunflower and sesame seeds, nuts, Green leafy vegetables, pulses, soya flour, meat, offal, egg yolk	Essential for the proper metabolism of starch and sugars. Important for the health of the skin, hair, muscles, nerves, eyes and blood
B2 Riboflavin	Wholegrain cereals, brewer's yeast, offal, nuts, seeds, fish, meat, dairy produce, eggs, potatoes, green leafy vegetables, pulses	
B3 Niacin	Wholegrain cereals, brewer's yeast, nuts, seeds, offal, meats, fish, pulses, soya flour, green leafy vegetables, mushrooms, dried apricots	
B6 Pyridoxin	Wholegrain cereals, wheatgerm, fish, brewer's yeast, pulses, soya flour, liver, chicken, walnuts, peanuts, bananas	
Vitamin B12	Liver, dairy food and other animal produce, fortified foods, yeast extracts, traces found in fermented soya bean products and seaweeds. The best sources are found in animal foods	Essential for red blood cell formation and integrity of nerve cells. Diets excluding all animal produce may need dietary supplements
Folic Acid	Wholegrain cereals, pulses, soya flour, offal, green leafy vegetables, mushrooms, egg yolk, oranges, brewer's yeast, potatoes, cow's milk	It is important to include this nutrient in preparation for and during pregnancy
Vitamin C **Ascorbic acid**	Fresh fruit especially berries and citrus fruits, green leafy vegetables, bean sprouts and seed sprouts, tomatoes, potatoes, melons, lacto-fermented cabbage (sauerkraut)	Increases resistance to infection. Encourages tissue repair and normal growth
Minerals **Calcium**	Sesame seeds, tahini, cheeses, milk, blackstrap molasses, seaweeds, sunflower seeds, almonds, green leafy vegetables, pulses, soya flour, carob, yoghurt, dried fruit, Japanese twig tea, brewer's yeast, tinned salmon, sardines	Needed for building bones and teeth. Involved in blood clotting. Important for heart function and health of the skin. See vitamin D function

THE SOURCE AND FUNCTION OF NUTRIENTS

NUTRIENT	SOURCES	FUNCTION
Iron	Brewer's yeast, blackstrap molasses, liver, seaweeds, sesame seeds, wholegrain cereals, green leafy vegetables, dried fruits, red meats, pulses, soya flour, egg yolk, sardines	Essential for blood formation. The absorption of iron is aided by foods containing vitamin C
Magnesium	Nuts, seeds, wholegrain cereals, dried fruits, soya beans, pulses, brewer's yeast, fruits, vegetables	Required for proper metabolism of carbohydrate. Involved in bone and teeth formation
Phosphorus	Usually present with calcium	Required with calcium for formation of bones and teeth
Potassium	Fruits, vegetables, seaweeds, pulses, soya flour, wholegrain cereals, nuts, seeds, brewer's yeast, blackstrap molasses, meat, fish	Essential for growth and the proper function of the heart
Sodium	Table salt, sea salt, miso, tamari and shoyu soya sauce, celery, meats, cheeses, nuts, egg yolk, dairy produce	Sodium is involved in many of the vital body processes but dietary sodium in the form of salt is best excluded in the first year and restricted from 1 to 7 years
Sulphur	Wholegrain cereals, pulses, soya flour, almonds, meat, eggs	Important for the health of the hair and nails
Trace elements **Zinc**	Nuts, seeds, meats, fish, shellfish, egg yolk, poultry, dairy produce, brewer's yeast, wholegrain cereals, yellow and green vegetables especially peas and yellow fruits like papaya and mango	A vital component of several enzymes concerned with digestion of carbohydrate and protein. Essential for normal growth and healing
Iodine	Sea foods, seaweeds, fish liver oils, pulses, soya flour, green vegetables, iodised salt, garlic	Essential for proper metabolism controlled by the thyroid gland which requires iodine for its proper function
Manganese	Wholegrain cereals, rice, wheat and oat germs, nuts, vegetables, pulses, soya flour, liver, berries	Essential for the utilization of vitamin B1. Aids reproduction and lactation

Eat in moderation

Eating in moderation requires an understanding of what moderation means for the individual. Most people can think of someone else who eats more than they do but the point is you should only eat as much as you need to satisfy your hunger. When eating fresh wholefoods it is easier to recognize when you have eaten sufficient for both appetite and body needs. Because they are lacking in fibre (bulk), it is all too easy to overeat refined foods without feeling full so avoid snacks which blunt the appetite for proper meals and avoid two and three course main meals and large evening snacks after 8 p.m. This will give your digestive system a chance to process the food properly before you go to bed, otherwise the result could be chronic indigestion, disturbed sleep and possibly a gradual increase in weight. Poor appetite at breakfast is often the result and this starts a pattern of missed meals and faulty eating.

When to feed children

The best times for meals are as follows:

Breakfast
6.30 a.m. – 9.30 a.m.

Lunch
12 noon – 1.30 p.m.

Tea
4.00 p.m. – 5.00 p.m.

Supper
6.00 p.m. – 8.00 p.m.

For the same reasons, it is better to give older babies and young children their main meals earlier in the day – at breakfast and lunch time rather than at night. There may be little scientific proof that cheese causes nightmares but any high fat, high protein food could, if improperly digested, cause a digestive upset which, during sleep, might become part of a dream or nightmare. If a child has a tendency to bedwetting it is best not to give large glasses of water or fruit drinks at bedtime. Do not restrict fluid but give it earlier in the day, between meals, and avoid feeding dry, highly seasoned or sweet foods, which will create thirst, just before bedtime.

Although many adolescents and adults do not bother with breakfast it is essential for young children to have a nourishing meal first thing in the morning. Therefore, it would be sensible for older members of the family to make time for it too, as it provides energy and stamina for the day and makes mid-morning snacks unnecessary.

For young children lunch time usually involves only one parent and seeing you eat the same or similar food is one of the best ways of teaching good eating habits. Time is needed at this meal to chat and have fun as well as eat.

A young child's tea between 4.00 p.m. and 5.00 p.m. followed by bed between 6.00 p.m. and 7.00 p.m. leaves the early evening free for the adult meal. This, comprising a main course of animal or vegetable protein with wholegrains and vegetables, provides the chief contribution to the daily nutrient needs, and a chance for adults and older children to unwind and share news. When both parents are working, a great deal of advance preparation and mutual co-operation is required if convenience foods are not to become dietary staples.

Parents will find they have more energy and stamina if they join their children in a nourishing breakfast

What to eat and what to avoid

It has already been said that a healthy, well-balanced diet is one which satisfies the body's nutrient needs and these will of course differ depending on whether we are talking about a farm labourer, an office clerk or a nursing mother, a growing child or a newborn baby. However, in the chart opposite, there is a suggested pattern of one week's healthy eating for an average, active adult, and at the end of the section there is a list of suggestions about foods to avoid if you want to ensure that your body will be supplied with all the nutrients it needs in balanced amounts.

A WEEK'S MENUS FOR HEALTHY ADULTS

DAY	BREAKFAST	LIGHT MEAL	MAIN MEAL
1	Barley and rye scones with apple sauce	Carrot purée soup Lentil paté with mung bean sprouts on mixed grain toast	Nut roast or roast chicken Oat and onion stuffing with roast jacket potato and Brussels sprouts Apricot kanten
2	Oat and barley porridge	Miso or chicken and buckwheat noodle broth Chinese leaves, tomato and watercress salad with baked jacket potato	Bean loaf or minced beef with turnips and steamed cabbage Glass mixed vegetable juice
3	Porridge or home-made muesli	Lentil Soup Slice of millet, carrot and leek bake Blanched broccoli with yoghurt, dill and apple cider vinegar dressing	Tofu scramble or herb omelette and braised celery with shallow fry potatoes or stir-fry brown rice Fresh or poached pear
4	Porridge or granola	Split pea and barley broth Carrot, beetroot and alfalfa salad with toasted sunflower seeds and almonds	Grilled fish or portion of aduki beans on basmatti rice with casserole of mixed vegetables in arrowroot sauce Portion of lacto-fermented pickles such as sauerkraut
5	Porridge or natural yoghurt with sesame seed meal and seasonal, fresh fruit	Split pea and leek soup Brown rice mixed with toasted, flaked hazelnuts Shredded cabbage with apple, raisins, spring onions and yoghurt dressing	Millet, sesame and vegetable bake with chickpea sauce and optional lamb chop Baked apple
6	Slice home-baked bread, toasted and spread with sunflower spread or no-sugar jam	Cauliflower purée Chickpea rissoles with brown rice and sweetcorn, red pepper and spring onion salad	Shallow fried fish with eating apple slices and French beans or Boston style beans on rye toast Fresh grapes
7	Porridge or soaked, dried fruit and sesame seed meal	Miso mushroom consommé Bean, nut or beefburger in a wholewheat roll with lettuce and tomato salad	Stir-fry brown rice with bean sprouts, shrimps, tofu or meat Steamed cauliflower greens and shoyu ginger dip Raisin and apple pie or mixed fruit

TABLE OF FOODS TO AVOID

The following foods are highly unsuitable for adults if taken in excess – in other words on a daily basis – and their restriction for children is strongly recommended. Of course, many apparently healthy children have been fed on some or all of these foods and it is up to parents to decide what their children shall eat but what we eat and drink can often take years to show its effect upon individual health so it is nutritionally wise to avoid them where possible.

Intensively reared and highly processed meat, fish and poultry
It is possible that these foods can contain traces of certain hormones used to speed growth, plus antibiotics and other medications to prevent and treat diseases of animals raised in large numbers in close proximity to each other. Additives like meat tenderizers and preservatives are also common ingredients.

Pork and pork products – ham, bacon, gammon, luncheon meat, sausages, patés and pies
Next to battery chickens and factory farmed veal, pork is the most highly processed and intensively reared of meats. Traditional methods of curing and smoking pork have been superseded by chemical processes. Pork products are high in both salt and nitrites (which, when converted in the body to nitrosamines have been found to raise the risk of cancer), while sausages, patés and pies are also high in fat, spices and wheat starch.

Meat broths, stocks and extracts, powders and stock cubes
The comments above apply similarly to the stock of those meats. Check ingredients' lists and eliminate those high in salt and containing monosodium glutamate, hydrolysed vegetable protein and artificial colouring and flavouring.

Salt and spices including curry powder, mustard, nutmeg, and pepper
The unsuitability of salt for babies and young children is discussed in Appendix I, Glossary of foods (see page 115). Salt and spices can damage the liver and kidneys.

Tinned and packet foods containing artificial colourings, flavourings, preservatives and other additives, refined sugar and salt
Adult convenience foods are too highly seasoned and flavoured for infant tastes although many babies will eat them and as a result refuse the more bland but more nourishing home-made meals. Some children are so badly affected by certain colourings and other additives that their behaviour is adversely affected making them aggressive and disruptive (see hyperactivity in Chapter 6).
Some commercial baby foods are available free of these additives.
Check ingredients.

Refined white flour and non-organic wheat flour and products – see wheat list
The importance of fibre is discussed in the Glossary of foods (see page 114) and noted in the Nutrient chart. It appears that the sensitivity to wheat and wheat products shown by many people suffering from conditions as variable as rheumatoid arthritis, palpitations, overweight, lack of energy and digestive problems could be the result of the use of artificial fertilizers and pesticides or the artificial bleaching agents found in commercial wheat flour and breads. If using wheat as flour, flakes or wholegrains the choice of organically/bio-dynamically grown wheat is advised. A sensitivity to wheat as described above is different from a gluten-sensitivity known as Coeliac disease (see page 102).

TABLE OF FOODS TO AVOID

Refined white and brown sugars and food and drinks containing them including sweets, squashes, jams, syrups, desserts, tinned soups and other savouries
Sugar should never be added to a baby's food or drinks. These concentrated sweeteners dull the appetite for real foods, can lead to overweight and a craving for sweet foods which upsets the general balance of health and increases proneness to infection and tooth decay. Check all ingredients' lists including baby foods, baby drinks, rusks and savouries. Do not be misled by claims such as 'This product contains no artificial sweetener'. Avoid all products which list sugar or sucrose, dextrose or glucose (the same thing), fructose, syrup, corn syrup, glucose syrup. Raw and unrefined sugars should also be avoided in the first 2 years and then used only sparingly, if at all, as an occasional treat in home baking or desserts.

Honey – avoid before 12 months (see page 115)
Although just as addictive and tooth threatening as the sugars, honey can be used sparingly after the first 12 months. Choose pure flower honey avoiding waxy, sugary imitations.

Alcoholic drinks, carbonated and sweetened drinks
The reasons for avoiding alcohol should be obvious. In countries where wine drinking is the norm there has been recent concern over a possible link between the high incidence of adult alcoholism and the giving of diluted wine to children. Carbonated drinks can cause painful gastric distention and sweetened drinks, especially when given in bottles, dummies, soothers and feeders result in prolonged contact of sugar with the teeth and subsequent decay. Many baby juices contain sugar. Check labels carefully.

Glucose drinks, coffee, tea, cocoa, drinking chocolate, cola and similar stimulant drinks
All these drinks contain the stimulant substance caffeine which if consumed by a baby, child or many adults can increase excitability and cause sleep disturbance. The additional inclusion of sugar also makes them unsuitable for reasons already stated.

Whole nuts, salted and commercially dry roasted nuts, potato crisps, salted crackers and popcorn
Whole nuts are a danger as they can be swallowed and cause choking. The salt, additives and high fat content of the other foods in this group exclude these snacks from a healthy diet. Home-made versions of toasted flaked nuts and seeds, potato sticks and popcorn can be simply and cheaply made for older children (see recipes).

Deep fried foods
The overheating of oils and fats which occurs in deep frying changes the structure of the fatty acids and causes nutrient imbalance making foods cooked in this way potentially harmful and difficult to digest. The frequent consumption of fried food can, in addition, lead to overweight. Lower temperature stir-frying using the minimum of oil is much preferred for adults and children.

Smoked fish, meats and cheeses
The smoking process introduces substances which can be potentially harmful if consumed regularly or in large amounts. The high salt content of many smoked foods also excludes their use for babies or young children. Much smoked fish, such as smoked haddock, contains colour dyes. Where possible buy fish smoked by traditional methods.

2 From 0 to 6 months

Newborn babies are so tiny, vulnerable and dependent on their parents for survival it is difficult not to worry about whether they are growing and thriving during the first months of life.

Almost all babies lose a few ounces after birth and as hospitals are loath to allow mothers home until their baby has regained its birthweight it is hardly surprising that a great deal of the parents' attention is concentrated on how well their baby is feeding – whether it be by breast or bottle.

Breastfeeding

Every mother produces the ideal food, in composition and consistency, for her newborn infant. Balanced in nutrients and protective factors, this instant baby food rivals in sophistication any man-made, computer-devised product.

The first milk or pre-milk, a clear fluid known as colostrum, is produced just after birth. Colostrum carries protective factors to the baby which lower the risk of present infection and future illness. All babies should be given the opportunity to receive this highly beneficial substance as their very first food. If you are planning to breastfeed, nursing and medical staff at your maternity hospital should be advised of your wishes that no substance (other than water or your own breast milk) be given to your baby except in an emergency situation. The giving of glucose or formula milk to a newborn infant to enable the mother to sleep, can sabotage her attempts to get breastfeeding fully established and have long-term repercussions regarding food intolerance when weaning starts.

Diet while breastfeeding

The diet and lifestyle of the breastfeeding mother prior to, during and after pregnancy, and the support she receives from the child's father, family and friends are all important in determining whether she will be able to produce sufficient milk for her baby's needs in its first 4 to 6 months of life.

To ensure an adequate milk supply it is important to drink plenty of fluids (preferably water) and to eat a good supply of protein foods, wholegrains and fresh vegetables. Eliminate refined and processed foods, artificial additives and stimulants such as alcohol and caffeine drinks and avoid smoking or drug-taking as all these can affect the new baby.

Breastfeeding gives your baby a perfectly balanced diet for the first 6 months of life

MENUS FOR EXPECTANT AND NURSING MOTHERS

DAY 1

Breakfast
Oat and barley flake porridge with toasted almond flakes

Lunch
Brown rice and shrimps with steamed greens

Evening meal
Lamb or bean stew with wholegrains or potatoes and a lightly cooked fresh vegetable

Mid-morning snack
Carrot, beetroot and celery salad with apple and toasted sunflower seeds

Mid-afternoon snack
Wineglass amount of freshly pressed or bottled mixed vegetable juice – carrot, celery, beetroot

Evening snack
Home-popped corn

DAY 2

Breakfast
Granola and apple purée

Lunch
Fine crêpes with bean sprout and egg, cheese or bean filling

Evening meal
One-pot poached fish and vegetables with parsley sauce

Mid-morning snack
Natural yoghurt and coleslaw salad (shredded cabbage, carrot, spring onion)

Mid-afternoon snack
Fresh peach

Evening snack
Toasted, unsalted nuts and seeds

DAY 3

Breakfast
Natural yoghurt and sesame seed meal with apricot purée and muesli

Lunch
Open sandwich on mixed grain bread with chicken liver or lentil and mushroom paté

Evening meal
Roast chicken or chicken and bean casserole on brown rice with braised celery

Mid-morning snack
Mung bean sprout and alfalfa salad

Mid-afternoon snack
Fresh apricots

Evening snack
Cottage cheese and herbs on crispbread

DAY 4

Breakfast
Buckwheat pancakes and cottage cheese

Lunch
Tofu and herb omelette

Evening meal
Grilled oily fish with cucumber and dill salad and apple cider vinegar dressing

Mid-morning snack
Rye crispbread with celery and sauerkraut salad

Mid-afternoon snack
Cantaloupe melon

Evening snack
Sesame or sunflower seed spread on crispbread

DAY 5

Breakfast
Scrambled egg on rye toast with mustard cress

Lunch
Cottage cheese with walnuts and seasonal salad or vegetable casserole

Evening meal
Bean or meat loaf with yeast extract sauce, steamed greens and carrots and barley rice

Mid-morning snack
Blanched broccoli and brown rice with flaked toasted hazelnuts

Mid-afternoon snack
Fresh berries – strawberries, raspberries, blackcurrants

Evening snack
Slices of baked sweet potato or steamed parsnip

DAY 6

Breakfast
Oatcakes and sunflower seed spread

Lunch
Bean or meat and vegetable pasties

Evening meal
Casserole of white fish with carrots, leek, fennel and potato topping

Mid-morning snack
Green leafy salad (Chinese leaves, lettuce, watercress, landcress, alfalfa)

Mid-afternoon snack
Fresh pear

Evening snack
Wineglass of lacto-fermented vegetable juice

DAY 7

Breakfast
Brown rice porridge with sultanas

Lunch
Millet bake with sliced avocado or lentil sauce

Evening meal
Minced beef or nut rissoles, baked jacket potato and seasonal salad

Mid-morning snack
Brown rice cake (puffed rice biscuit) and carrot spread

Mid-afternoon snack
Fresh grapes

Evening snack
Crunchy lettuce leaves filled with yoghurt and white cheese or bean sprout, apple and celery filling

TIPS

☐ Pregnancy sickness – starting the day with a raw apple or sips of unsweetened apple juice, a few raisins or dry crispbread can help alleviate symptoms – keep these beside the bed. ☐ Although a fat store is laid down during pregnancy to act as an energy source during breastfeeding, energy needs will be much greater at this time (by about 600–800 calories a day). Six, small nourishing meals are often a better way to supply these needs than one or two main meals. ☐ There is a general increase in thirst, often whilst breastfeeding, so keep a jug of water beside you at this time but do not force yourself to drink more than you wish. Fluid in excess of 3 litres (6 pints) has been shown to diminish milk supply. ☐ There is no need to drink milk (see Nutrient chart for other calcium sources). Water, unsweetened fruit juice and other non-stimulant drinks are more thirst quenching. ☐ Keeping meals to simple mixtures of compatible foods is easier on the digestion and, particularly in the early stages of breastfeeding, makes any upsets in the baby easier to trace if linked to the mother's diet. ☐ Avoid raw onion or garlic and too much fruit as these things can sometimes upset the baby's digestion.

Breastfeeding and drugs

If a need arises for the mother to take medication whilst breastfeeding, professional advice is required to confirm whether breastfeeding should stop, or whether, on balance, it would be better for the mother to get by without the drug if possible. Unknown factors such as the effect of vaccination for foreign travel upon the composition of breast milk advises caution.

There are very few cases in which breastfeeding is impossible or where there is not enough milk for at least the first 3 to 4 months. The advice and support of a well-qualified maternity nurse is invaluable and most mothers have the opportunity of attending classes throughout pregnancy which will prepare them for breastfeeding.

Increased knowledge removes fears and worries that result in unnecessary failure. Any possible objections tend to disappear when an explanation is given of the role of breast milk and the dual benefits to mother and baby. Although it may take a few weeks to get breastfeeding fully established mothers unable to breastfeed are a rare occurrence when their way of eating is based on fresh, whole produce as outlined here. The first 5 to 6 months of a baby's life should, therefore, present no problems with regards to catering.

Choosing not to breastfeed

Social pressures are one of the main reasons why some mothers choose not to breastfeed their babies. Some women or their partners feel shy about exposing their breasts in public; some may be planning to return to work in the near future; others may not have an adequate supply of milk to satisfy their baby's needs or feel that because their babies are finding it a little difficult to suck at first, they would be better on a bottle. This is sometimes the case with premature babies who can be slow feeders but if they are encouraged to suckle regularly, at short intervals, the milk supply will soon increase.

Whatever the reason, if a mother decides not to breastfeed she must not feel that she is failing her baby. If she has been able to breastfeed for even a few weeks she will already have passed on many benefits but even if this has not been possible, careful bottlefeeding will also result in a happy, healthy infant.

Bottlefeeding

Bottlefeeding is no easy way out – quite the opposite. Success requires careful selection of the right milk, equipment and feeding techniques. Bottlefed babies need just as much cuddling and encouragement as breastfed babies and it is both dangerous and thoughtless to leave a baby to bottlefeed himself.

Choose one of the specially formulated baby milk powders and always use the scoop which is provided and follow the

Bottlefed babies need plenty of cuddling and encouragement and should never be left to feed themselves

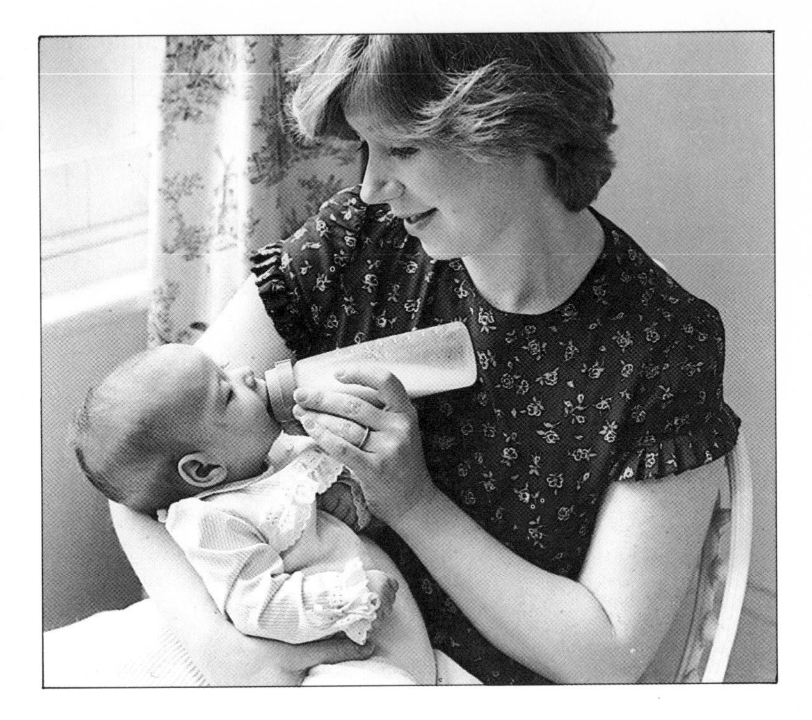

mixing instructions very carefully. Never add an extra scoop as too concentrated a feed can cause kidney damage. All feeding equipment should be sterilized before use either by boiling for thirty minutes or soaking in a special sterilizing solution. Always rinse soaked equipment very thoroughly, with boiled water, to remove traces of solution and use boiled, cooled water to mix with the formula milk.

Crying does not always mean hunger so check if your baby needs to be changed or is thirsty for a drink of boiled, cooled water or is simply bored, before giving a bottle of formula milk. Studies have shown that bottlefed babies are more prone to overweight than those who are breastfed so let your baby decide when he has had enough – don't try to coax him to take more and don't be tempted to start introducing solids too early; as with breastfed babies, wait until he is at least 4 months old.

Diet for mothers who are bottlefeeding

Eating well is just as important if you are bottlefeeding your baby. Choose lower calorie, nutrient-rich foods to encourage the loss of weight gained during pregnancy. Avoid all fried and fatty foods, refined sweet and starchy foods and sweetened drinks, at least until your ideal weight is achieved. A starvation diet is not the answer as a daily supply of nutrients is needed to provide stamina for the busy days ahead and to help you emotionally and physically after the birth.

Alternative milks

The table below shows the comparative compositions of four milks each designed for specific purposes. Cows have a larger bone structure than humans and bone development is of vital importance for the calf, hence the high protein and calcium content in cow's milk. As well as extra protein there is also extra sodium in cow's milk which is undesirable for babies whose immature kidneys are unable to handle a sodium excess. Goat's milk is low in the B group vitamin, folic acid, which is essential for proper blood formation and although it is more suitable for babies with regard to protein, calcium and sodium content, it should not be used exclusively for infants without careful supplementation. Because the intolerance of some infants to cow's milk has led to the use of goat's milk as an alternative, intolerance to goat's milk can also occur but if it is tolerated and supplemented care must be taken to obtain goat's milk from disease-free herds. Modified soya milk (not the regular dried or tinned versions) has a nutrient content very similar to mother's milk but, despite this, allergies to it can occur. Cow's milk-sensitive babies often require that their mothers avoid all dairy produce while they are breastfeeding.

COMPOSITION OF MILKS

NUTRIENTS/100 g MILK	BREAST MILK	COW'S MILK	GOAT'S MILK	SOYA MILK*
Energy (calories)	69	65	71	67
Protein (g)	1.3	3.3	3.3	2
Fat (g)	4.1	3.8	4.5	3.6
Carbohydrate (g)	7.2	4.7	4.6	6.6
Sodium (mg)	14	50	40	20
Potassium (mg)	58	150	180	64.5
Calcium (mg)	34	120	130	55
Iron (mg)	0.07	0.05	0.04	1.2
Vitamin A (micro g)	60	35	40	50.7
Vitamin D (micro g)	0.025	0.03	0.06	1.05
Thiamin (mg)	0.02	0.04	0.04	0.05
Riboflavin (mg)	0.03	0.19	0.15	0.06
Nicotinic Acid (mg)	0.22	0.08	0.19	0.8
Pyridoxin (mg)	0.01	0.04	0.04	0.04
Biotin (micro g)	0.7	2.0	2.0	5
Vitamin C (mg)	3.7	1.5	1.5	5.4
Vitamin E (mg)	0.34	0.1	n/a	1.5
Folic Acid (micro g)	n/a	18	n/a	10

*Fortified soya milk or soya milk formula *NOT* cartons or tins of soya milk.

How much to feed

Views on infant feeding have changed drastically over the years. Current thought includes the opinion that a healthy baby is the best judge of how often and how much he or she requires nourishment. Low birthweight babies may need some encouragement to feed. Premature babies who are often too weak to suckle from the breast can benefit from their mother's milk if it is expressed and put into a bottle. Unfortunately, breastfeeding can involve more work for the baby, particularly if it is small or premature, than bottlefeeding. Therefore, babies who have been offered bottlefeeds before breastfeeds are often reluctant to come off the bottle! If the mother is nervous about breastfeeding she will invariably transmit these feelings to her baby who may then refuse to feed. Advance preparation and thoughtful professional support will help eliminate any fears and ensure good results. It will probably take several weeks before a successful pattern is established.

Establishing a routine

Although advice is often given not to wake a child for a feed, care must be taken to ensure sufficient nourishment is being taken for normal growth. Traditionally babies feed every four hours, but many babies might want to be fed more frequently – every three or even two hours. In the first few weeks, it is best to be guided by your baby. Feed him on demand and gradually you will find some kind of pattern emerging with the baby probably only expecting to be fed six or seven times a day; although sometimes when he has growth spurts (often at 6 or 12 weeks) he might demand another feed unexpectedly.

In the first six weeks regular suckling is important, both to supply the rapidly growing baby with sufficient nourishment and to stimulate the mother's milk supply, but after this time many mothers find their babies drop the late evening or night feed and sleep for a longer stretch. From about 6 to 8 weeks, a larger interval between feeds is important to allow proper digestion of the previous meal, although in the early stages it is equally important not to let the gap extend for too long a period even though your baby appears to be contented to continue sleeping. Soon you will know your own baby's needs and be able to monitor both growth and development.

Introducing solids

How can you tell if your baby is ready to be weaned? There is no exact age at which you should start adding solids to a milk diet – every baby is different. But at some point, probably between 4 and 6 months, you will notice your baby's appetite increasing. By 6 to 8 months most babies will be ready to eat solids and nutritionally there are a number of good reasons why it is important not to feed your baby exclusively on milk (breast or

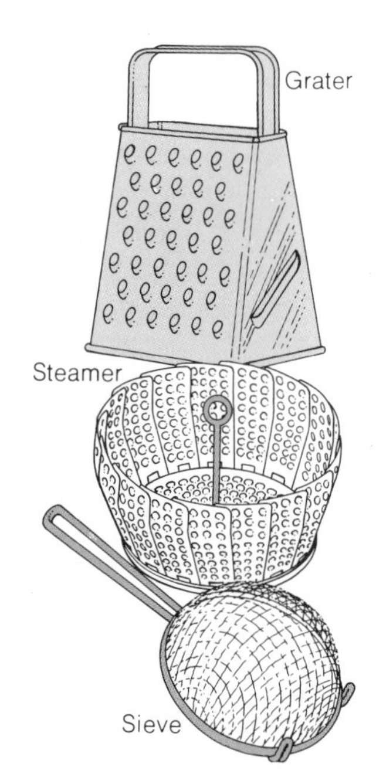

formula) beyond this time. One of the main reasons is that milk alone supplies inadequate amounts of the mineral iron for the baby's growing needs.

Basically, the fresh, nutritionally balanced, wholefood diet which was outlined in Chapter 1, provides all your baby's needs as well as those of the rest of the family. When you first introduce solids, it is best, easiest and cheapest to adapt the food the rest of the family are eating. Cook the basics for the regular meal but without any seasoning. Purée or sieve some of the food for the baby and then season the main part for the adults and older children. When teeth appear you can give mashed and eventually chopped foods. The Weaning chart and the Weaning menu suggestions (see page 36) will help you decide in what order to introduce foods as your baby progresses on to a fully mixed diet, although the exact age you find most suitable for him may not always correspond with the ages given on the charts.

When solids are accepted, gradually increase the amounts until they replace milk as the baby's staple diet. Start with only tiny tastes of food and even as appetite increases still offer very small portions as the baby's digestive system can only gradually learn to adjust to the new diet. Do not get carried away by

your baby's enthusiasm in the first few weeks of introducing solids. He might adore puréed pear and want to eat six or eight spoonfuls but his digestive system is not yet ready to cope so it is important to offer only one or two teaspoonfuls at a time and gradually increase the amounts.

Some babies enjoy being encouraged to eat and feeding time can be a long and fun-filled process. Always allow plenty of time for meals with your baby because it is very important to be patient and to go at the baby's pace. Adults generally eat much too fast and the inclination is to try and hurry the baby too. Other babies show little interest in solid foods until they are over 6 months and as long as they are thriving on breast or formula milk there is nothing to be gained by trying to force your baby on to other foods.

Ideas about when to start weaning vary from generation to generation but current thinking argues against the introduction of solids earlier than 4 months and one of the main reasons is because early weaning has been implicated as a cause of food allergy (see Chapter 6 for further information).

When to avoid weaning

It is best to avoid weaning during the hottest weeks of the year because one of the things a breastfeeding mother must do during weaning is reduce her milk supply by cutting down on her own liquid consumption. This is difficult to do during hot weather and could be harmful to the mother if she became dehydrated.

It is also advisable to avoid weaning when travelling because the excitement and uncertainty generated in the baby by the change in environment often results in him wanting and needing the reassurance and comfort of sucking. If this is denied him it could cause distress. Furthermore, when travelling it might also be difficult to get access to suitable foods and preparation facilities (see Chapter 5 for further hints on travelling).

Lastly, it is inadvisable to wean during any acute phase of teething.

First foods

Different communities in different countries have their own traditions about what should be the first foods to introduce to babies. Some people suggest cereal as it is bland and if mixed with a little breast or formula milk tastes similar to what the baby is already used to. Others suggest a little puréed fruit or vegetable because the totally new taste can often surprise and excite the baby and, as at this stage all solid food is extra to the full complement of milk feeds which he will still be having, there is no possibility of excess weight gain as fruits and vegetables are low in calories.

When you give your baby his first taste of food put only a tiny amount on the tip of a teaspoon so he can suck it off

Favourite first tastes include half a teaspoon of freshly grated carrot juice which has been squeezed through a fine muslin; puréed steamed cauliflower or parsnip; lightly boiled, puréed pear or apple; cereal gruels and soft cooked millet.

Try introducing foods at the mid-day or evening feed or whenever your baby seems most hungry. Your baby will already have had one milk feed and any disruption caused by the new routine will not result in a serious reduction in milk intake. Offer a half to one teaspoon of, for instance, special baby rice (see page 39) before the breastfeed. Use only the tip of the spoon and place in front of the baby's mouth so he can 'suck' it off. Never try to deposit food on to his tongue or right inside his mouth. At first the feel of the spoon and the unexpected taste of the cereal may cause your carefully prepared offering to be rejected. If it does, do not force the issue but simply try again the next day. Gradually increase the amount of food from one to four teaspoons over the next week.

When one food is well tolerated introduce the next in the same way progressing from fine, almost liquid gruels to lightly textured, soft feeds. The time spent at each stage will vary according to your baby. Some babies require coaxing on to more textured foods but at no time should they be rushed on to the next stage before they are completely ready – physically or emotionally. Smooth, bland food will soon lose its appeal when teeth appear.

Start your baby on almost liquid gruels and slowly progress to lightly textured purées. Never rush from one stage to the next – let him dictate the pace

Weaning Hints

Here are a few tips to remember when weaning.

□ Take it gently and gradually.

□ Introduce only one new food at a time.

□ Do not try new foods when your baby is over-hungry, tired or suffering acute teething problems.

□ At the first feed only offer a teaspoonful. If food is rejected try again a few days later. You can trust your baby's preference provided you are offering the right foods. If babies are fed on highly sweetened products, they will reject the subtler sweetness of nourishing root vegetables, grains and fruits.

□ Never add cereal or rusks to a bottle feed.

□ Do not feed juices, sweetened or unsweetened, in a bottle. Give in teaspoon amounts at first, well diluted. Special drinking beakers make the transition from breast or bottlefeeding easier, although it may take a few weeks to establish the drinking technique.

□ Be cautious when mixing fruit and vegetables or fresh fruit and grain mixtures at the same feed as the different speeds at which the foods are digested could cause stomach upsets.

□ Bedtime eating should always be discouraged except for very young babies. Some babies sleep better if they have a light cereal meal in the early evening, given as a spoonfeed.

□ Never leave your baby alone with food. It is very easy to choke when you cannot chew properly (see page 109 for what to do if your baby chokes).

□ Never give nuts or sweets as these can block the baby's windpipe.

□ Avoid re-heating leftovers, especially if they contain animal foods.

□ Never re-use tins or jars of food if the eating spoon has been dipped in them.

□ Give small portions of food and throw away leftovers.

□ Babies of small build may gain weight more slowly than others. Remember babies weaned firstly onto vegetable foods tend to be smaller and lighter than those weaned on to animal foods. Ask your health visitor or doctor if you are worried about your baby's weight.

□ If your baby is frequently irritable, wheezes, has rashes, loses weight or 'fails to thrive', this could be linked with a dietary problem such as a milk allergy (see page 107). Whether you suspect an allergy or not avoid introducing unmodified cow's milk until 12 months and avoid solids other than gluten-free grains (see page 113), cooked vegetables and fruit purées until over 6 months. Use only organically grown wheat.

□ Encourage self-feeding. Babies tending to overweight are more likely to eat only as much as they need this way.

WEANING MENU SUGGESTIONS

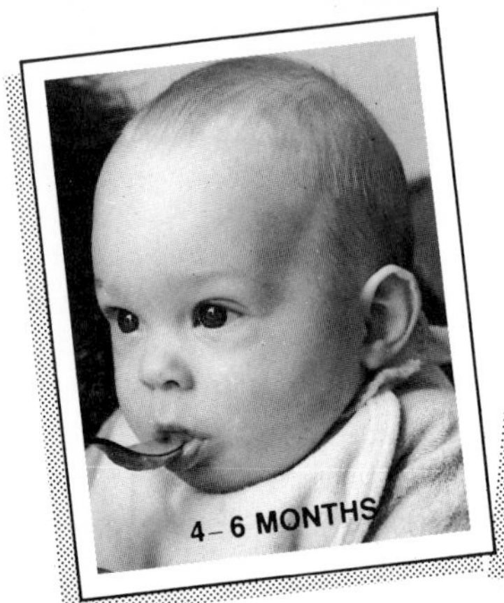

	4–6 MONTHS	6–8 MONTHS	8–12 MONTHS
ON WAKING	Breast or bottle feed	Breast or bottle feed	Water or well-diluted fresh vegetable or fruit juice
BREAKFAST	Breast or bottle feed	Special baby rice Breast or bottle feed	Wholegrain porridge made from one or more cereals Salt-free crispbread, puffed rice cake, wholegrain bread or home-made rusks Water, well-diluted fruit or vegetable juice
MID-DAY	Breast or bottle feed 1–2 tsp special baby rice	Breast or bottle feed 1–2 tsp rice or oat or barley or millet with puréed vegetable Sieved lentil or split pea broth	Minced or mashed pulses or fish, wholegrains and lightly steamed vegetables Ground rice creams or fruit desserts Water or diluted fresh vegetable juice
MID-AFTERNOON		Raw apple, carrot sticks or other teething food	Fresh fruit pieces
EARLY EVENING	Breast or bottle feed	Breast or bottle feed 1–2 tsp special baby rice with sesame seed meal	Mixed grain bread and savoury spread Raw cucumber sticks, blanched celery sticks and cauliflower florets Fresh fruit jelly Water, well-diluted apple juice or milk
BED-TIME	Breast or bottle feed	Breast or bottle feed	Water if required

WEANING CHART UP TO 24 MONTHS

AGE OF BABY IN MONTHS

	0	1	2	3	4	5	6	7	8	9	10	11	12	13	14	15	16	17	18	19	20	21	22	23	24
Milk: Mother's breast milk																									
Formula feed (soya or cow's milk)																									
Nut and seed milks																									
Goat's milk																									
Cow's milk																									
Water																									
Juices																									
Cereals: Brown rice, millet																									
Barley, oats, rye																									
Organic wholewheat, maize, buckwheat noodles																									
Baby foods																									
Fruit: Raw																									
Cooked																									
Dried																									
Teething foods																									
Cucumber																									
Salad leaves																									
Vegetables: Carrot, cauliflower, parsnip, pumpkin, swede, turnip																									
Celery, leafy greens, leeks, mushrooms, onion, squash																									
Bean sprouts																									
Potatoes																									
Fish																									
Pulses: Lentils, split peas, aduki beans																									
Chickpeas, kidney beans, haricot beans																									
Sweeteners																									
Seasonings: Herbs																									
Miso																									
Sea salt																									
Tofu																									
Yoghurt																									
Cheese: Cottage – home-made																									
Others																									
Honey																									
Bread																									
Oil																									
Butter																									
Eggs									Yolk only										Whole eggs						
Margarine																									
Pasta																									
Biscuits																									
Cake																									
Meat																									
Nuts and seeds																									
Sweet treats																									
Tomatoes																									
Sea vegetables: Dulse, nori, agar agar																									
Wakame, kombu, arame																									
Vitamin and mineral supplements – Check with doctor or health visitor																									

Gradual introduction or reduction of food from this age

Food can be used at this age

NB Chart is a guide only. Allowance must be for individual requirements.

Read *Appendix 1* Glossary of foods for a full explanation of chart (see page 110).

SESAME NUT MILK

(Serves 3–4)

25 g (1 oz) dehusked sesame seeds
50 g (2 oz) blanched almonds
350 ml (12 fl oz) water
15 g (½ oz) soaked sultanas

Blend nuts and seeds, then gradually add water and sweeten to taste with sultana soaking water. Do not use as a substitute for breast milk or formula feed.

FRUIT AND NUT MILK

(Makes one feed)

1 level tsp almond cream
1 tsp brown rice syrup or unrefined sugar (dark sugars may have too laxative an effect)
1 tbs tepid, boiled water
25 ml (1 fl oz) unsweetened apple and blackcurrant juice
hot boiled water to make up to 200–225 ml (7–8 fl oz)

Combine nut cream with sugar. Add tepid water one drop at a time, stirring to make a soft paste. Slowly dilute with hot water, then strain into feeding bottle. Add fruit juice and enough hot water to reach the required mark. Shake bottle to mix thoroughly and warm in a jug of hot water if using immediately. If not for immediate use do not add fruit juice until required.

This 'milk' is high in vitamin C and contains more iron than breast and animal milks. Use to supplement breast milk where there is a cow's milk intolerance. Give as a bottle feed after the breast feed, or use to replace one feed.

BROWN RICE MILK

(Makes 1 litre [2 pints])

100 g (4 oz) short grain brown rice
1 litre (2 pints) water

Bring rice to boil in water in a heavy covered pot. Simmer 2–3 hours. Strain through muslin.

The remaining 'milk' is very appealing to a young child, resembling mother's milk in taste and consistency, especially if a trace of brown rice syrup is added. Do not use as a substitute for breast milk or formula feed.

OATMILK

(From 5 months. Makes 570 ml [1 pint])

100 g (4 oz) whole oat groats
700 ml (24 fl oz) water
pinch sea salt (optional from 12 months)

Put oats, water and (salt) in a heavy pot, then bring to simmering, stirring gently. Cover and cook over a gentle heat for 1 hour or until oats are soft. Skim off the top liquid – this is the oatmilk – and use in any recipe requiring milk such as soups, sauces, desserts.

Do not use as a substitute for breast milk or formula feed.

OATCREAM

(From 5 months. Serves 3–4)

100 g (4 oz) whole oat groats
700 ml (24 fl oz) water
100 g (4 oz) soaked, dried apricots or 1 ripe peach, pear or eating apple

Follow recipe above to skimming stage then sieve oats and allow to cool. Meanwhile stew fruit in a little water for 5–10 minutes until soft. Cool and purée. Mix with sieved oats to make oatcream.

This makes an ideal first weaning food.

VEGETABLE NUTMILKS

(Serves 3–4)

225 ml (8 fl oz) nut, seed or soya milk
225 g (8 oz) carrots, steamed

Blend milk and vegetable then dilute as required.

25 g (1 oz) blanched almonds, finely ground
25 g (1 oz) celery
100 g (4 oz) carrots
25 g (1 oz) Chinese leaves
400 ml (14 fl oz) vegetable stock

Blend all ingredients and strain.

225 ml (8 fl oz) nut or seed milk
75 g (3 oz) beetroot, steamed
150 g (6 oz) carrot, steamed

Blend all ingredients, strain and dilute as required.

BABY MUESLI 1

(Serves 1)

1 heaped tsp oat flakes or fine oatmeal
1–2 tbs condensed milk or reconstituted baby milk powder
½ tsp nut cream
1 apple, freshly grated or sieved seasonal berries
2–3 drops fresh lemon juice

Soak flakes in milk and nut cream. Stir in fruit and lemon juice.

This makes a delicious breakfast cereal for a young baby.

BABY MUESLI 2

(Serves 1)

1 tsp fine oatmeal or
2 tsp oatflakes, soaked overnight in 2 tsp cold water
pinch oat germ
1 tsp almond cream
1 tsp lemon juice
1 tbs baby milk
1 small apple

Just before serving, finely grate apple and mix with other ingredients.

This may also be served as a porridge by heating through and adding a little water to moisten.

FRESH FRUIT PURÉE

(Serves 2)

100 g (4 oz) fresh fruit of choice or 75 g (3 oz) fresh fruit plus 25 g (1 oz) dried fruit
1–2 tbs water

If using dried fruit pre-soak to soften in a little hot water, then use soaking water to cook fruit. Place fruit in a suitable pot. Add water to moisten, then cover and simmer until soft. Allow to cool slightly before puréeing or mashing depending on the age of the baby or serve whole for older children.

Soft summer fruits such as strawberries, raspberries or soft peaches can be mashed without cooking but for easier digestion are best added to a kuzu, arrowroot or agar agar jelly (see page 58).

FORTIFIED GOAT'S MILK

(From 6 months. Makes 570 ml [1 pint])

570 ml (1 pint) goat's milk from accredited herd or the equivalent reconstituted powdered goat's milk
½ tsp brewer's yeast powder
½ tsp blackstrap molasses

Bring milk to boil and simmer for 2–3 minutes. Allow to cool to blood heat, then stir in yeast powder and molasses. Strain into sterilized bottle. If making larger amounts be sure that proportions are correct and that bottle ingredients are well mixed before serving.

The amount of brewer's yeast and molasses is correct for a baby of 6 months. Gradually increase to 1 tsp brewer's yeast and 1 tsp molasses by 8 months.

NB Goat's milk without the addition of brewer's yeast and molasses is unsuitable for babies as a replacement for mother's milk or modified cow's milk formula as it lacks the essential nutrient, folic acid, one of the B group vitamins needed for blood formation.

SPECIAL BABY RICE

(Serves 4)

75 g (3 oz) short grain brown rice
425 ml (15 fl oz) water

Wash the rice by swirling in a pot of water 2–3 times. Drain, then add measured amount of water and put in a pot with a tight-fitting lid. Cover and bring to the boil then simmer for 1–1½ hours until all water is absorbed and rice is creamy. For very young babies put the mixture through a freshly boiled muslin cloth.

This makes a light cereal which is easy to digest and you can use the remaining cereal to thicken adult soups or blend with a little barley malt or sultana juice to make a dessert for older children. Gradually reduce amount of water as appetite increases.

VEGETABLE RICE PURÉE

(Serves 3–4)

To the above recipe add 100 g (4 oz) of the following: diced carrot, turnip, pumpkin or squash. Cook with rice and sieve as required.

BARLEY RICE

(Serves 3–4)

50 g (2 oz) short grain brown rice
25 g (1 oz) pearl barley

Soak barley for 1 hour. Add to pot with rice and water as for Special baby rice and cook as before, sieving as required.

BROWN RICE CREAM

(Serves 4)

100 g (4 oz) short grain brown rice
570 ml (1 pint) water

Roast rice in a dry, heavy-bottomed pot until it begins to pop and is pale golden in colour. Cool, then blend or grind to a fine powder. Return powder to the pot and continue roasting gently to release a nutlike aroma. Bring water to the boil and gradually stir into rice flour. Bring mixture to the boil then simmer, cover and cook for 45 minutes. Stir to mix before serving.

As this is a flour product it is more likely to cause constipation and therefore is less preferable to whole or flaked grains.

SEA VEGETABLE STOCK

Take a piece of dried seaweed, brush off particles of sand and salt, place in a bowl and cover with fresh water. Allow to soak for 2–3 minutes. Remove seaweed, slice and add to casserole or soup. Strain soaking liquid through a muslin sieve to remove sand particles and add the liquid, which is rich in nutrients, to cooking.

KUZU SOUP

(Serves 1–2)

225 ml (8 fl oz) water, dulse or vegetable stock
25 g (1 oz) kuzu, dissolved in a little water

Bring water or stock to boil and stir in kuzu. Simmer until soup becomes clear. Remove from heat and add a few drops tamari soya sauce or serve without seasoning for babies under 18 months.

Kuzu is a gluten-free plant starch with thickening properties so it is particularly suited for weak digestions or after illness.

DULSE STOCK

(Serves 4)

15 cm (6 in) strip dulse
570 ml (1 pint) water

Simmer dulse in water for 15 minutes. This makes a stock rich in vitamins and minerals, which can be added to soups, casseroles and stews or used as a basis for sauces.

VEGETABLE BROTH

(From 4 months. Serves 4)

300 g (12 oz) carrots, diced
25 g (1 oz) brown rice or millet flakes
425 ml (15 fl oz) water

Cook carrots and flakes together in water until both are tender, then sieve. Gradually try other vegetables to vary the broth. Later a little cooked noodle (buckwheat) can be added in place of flaked grain.

STEAMED VEGETABLES

Carefully wash and slice greens. Keep smaller leaves whole to reduce nutrient loss.

Place leaves in steamer in a pot with 2.5 cm (1 in) water. Cover and steam for 3–10 minutes. If whole leaves have been used, shred just before serving.

Suitable vegetables include cauliflower, carrot, pumpkin, Brussels sprouts, (divide into leaves or make an incision in the base), Chinese leaves, turnip tops, radish tops.

NB Do not use potato leaves or rhubarb leaves as both of these are poisonous.

SEED AND NUT MEAL

(Serves 6–8)

225 g (8 oz) seeds or nuts (sesame, sunflower, pumpkin, almond, hazelnut, cashew, walnut)

Spread seeds evenly on baking sheet and toast under grill, stirring frequently to prevent burning. Allow to cool then grind to a fine meal. A batch of seeds or nuts can be toasted and ground as required to preserve nutrients. Use as toppings on porridge or in baking, casseroles and spreads.

A simple way of fortifying dishes with protein, calcium, trace elements and calories.

FIRST MEALS

Follow standard grain or pulse recipe (page 122) when cooking grains and pulses.
(Each meal serves 1)

1 tbs cooked oats, rice or barley + ½ tsp light tahini
1 tbs steamed cabbage, kale, broccoli or cauliflower
1 tbs steamed pumpkin, carrot, turnip or swede

Sieve, purée or mash depending on age and stage.

1 tbs cooked millet
1 tbs cooked mashed beans (aduki, lima, lentil)
1 tbs each steamed carrot and leek
2 tsp soya milk or nut milk

Blend milk with vegetables and serve with grain and beans or purée all ingredients.

1 tbs brown rice, soft cooked
½ tbs cooked brown or green lentils
1 tbs steamed squash or pumpkin
2 tsp kombu stock

Serve ingredients separately, with stock added to lentils, or blend all ingredients.

1 tbs brown rice and barley, soft cooked
½ tbs cooked black-eye beans
1 tbs steamed swede
¼ tsp kelp powder

Blend swede and kelp. Serve as above.

1 tbs oatflakes
1 tbs onion, very finely sliced
½ tbs dulse, shredded
½ tsp brewer's yeast powder (optional)
4–5 tbs vegetable stock

Simmer onion until soft. Add dulse and oatflakes and cook gently until grain is swollen adding more stock if required. Stir in brewer's yeast before serving, if used.

1 tbs buckwheat noodles, cooked
½ tbs cooked aduki beans
2–3 green beans, steamed
1 tbs kombu arrowroot sauce

Combine all ingredients in sauce.

1 tbs cooked brown rice
½ tbs cooked beans, black-eye or aduki
1 tbs steamed pumpkin
½ tbs kombu arrowroot sauce

Blend beans, vegetable and sauce. Serve with grain.

1 tbs brown rice
1 tbs green lentil sprouts steamed with
1 tbs shredded Brussels sprouts
1 tsp toasted flaked almonds

Combine rice and almonds, mashing or sieving, and serve with sprouts.

1 tbs cooked millet
1 tbs tofu
1 tbs steamed carrot
¼ tsp freshly chopped parsley

Mash tofu and vegetables. Serve with millet.

1 tbs cooked millet
1 tsp sesame seed meal
1 tbs steamed greens
1 tbs steamed carrots

Combine millet and sesame and serve with vegetables.

1 tbs cooked millet
1 tbs alfalfa sprouts
1 tbs carrot, very finely grated
1 tsp cooked aduki beans

Blend alfalfa, carrots and beans and serve with millet.

1 egg yolk, beaten (from 8 months)
2 tbs hot water
1 tbs steamed vegetables, finely shredded (spinach, turnip or radish tops, spring cabbage)

Combine egg and water. Scramble in oiled pot adding cooked vegetables and serve sieved or mashed depending on age of baby.

3 From 6 to 12 months

From weaning to solids

If you started introducing your baby to first food tastes at about 4 months and she responded enthusiastically, then by 6 months she will be ready to begin moving, in earnest, towards a fully mixed diet. Although at this stage the baby is probably still on four or five milk feeds a day, you will now be able to decrease them, and gradually, over the next three or four months cut them out altogether. This becomes increasingly necessary as the baby's nutrient requirements grow and her digestive track is able to cope with the changeover from a milk to a solid diet.

The 6 month stage is particularly suited for accelerated weaning because babies are, by now, usually sitting up by themselves and taking a much more active interest in their surroundings. This is the point at which it is advisable to get mealtimes organized; firstly, to minimize the mess, and secondly, to establish a routine that will enable the baby to participate in family eating patterns.

Mealtime equipment

Up to this point you probably gave your baby her first food tastes on your lap but if she can sit up it is advisable to secure her firmly in a highchair (see illustration); cover the floor with several large sheets of newspaper or a waterproof bath sheet (it is surprising how far food can fly!); and put a bib around her neck. The hard plastic kind with a pocket to catch food are practical for older babies but not suitable for younger babies; neither are they convenient if the highchair is the type where the table fits tightly to the baby's body. Soft plastic bibs with sleeves are obviously sensible but getting a tiny, wriggling, hungry baby's arms into them can sometimes be rather an ordeal. A conventional bib to protect the baby's front and her sleeves pulled up will probably suffice and it is best to accept that early on your baby can get very dirty during mealtimes.

Obviously a baby will not be able to cope with cutlery at this stage but always give her her own teaspoon to wave around. While she is struggling to put it into the dish you will be able to feed her with another teaspoon. Start using a teacher beaker for mealtime drinks. You will be surprised at how quickly she will learn to hold it for herself. There is no need to wean a breastfeeding baby on to a bottle if she will accept a beaker.

Weaning your baby on to nutritious whole-foods provides a sound basis for future health

MEALTIME EQUIPMENT

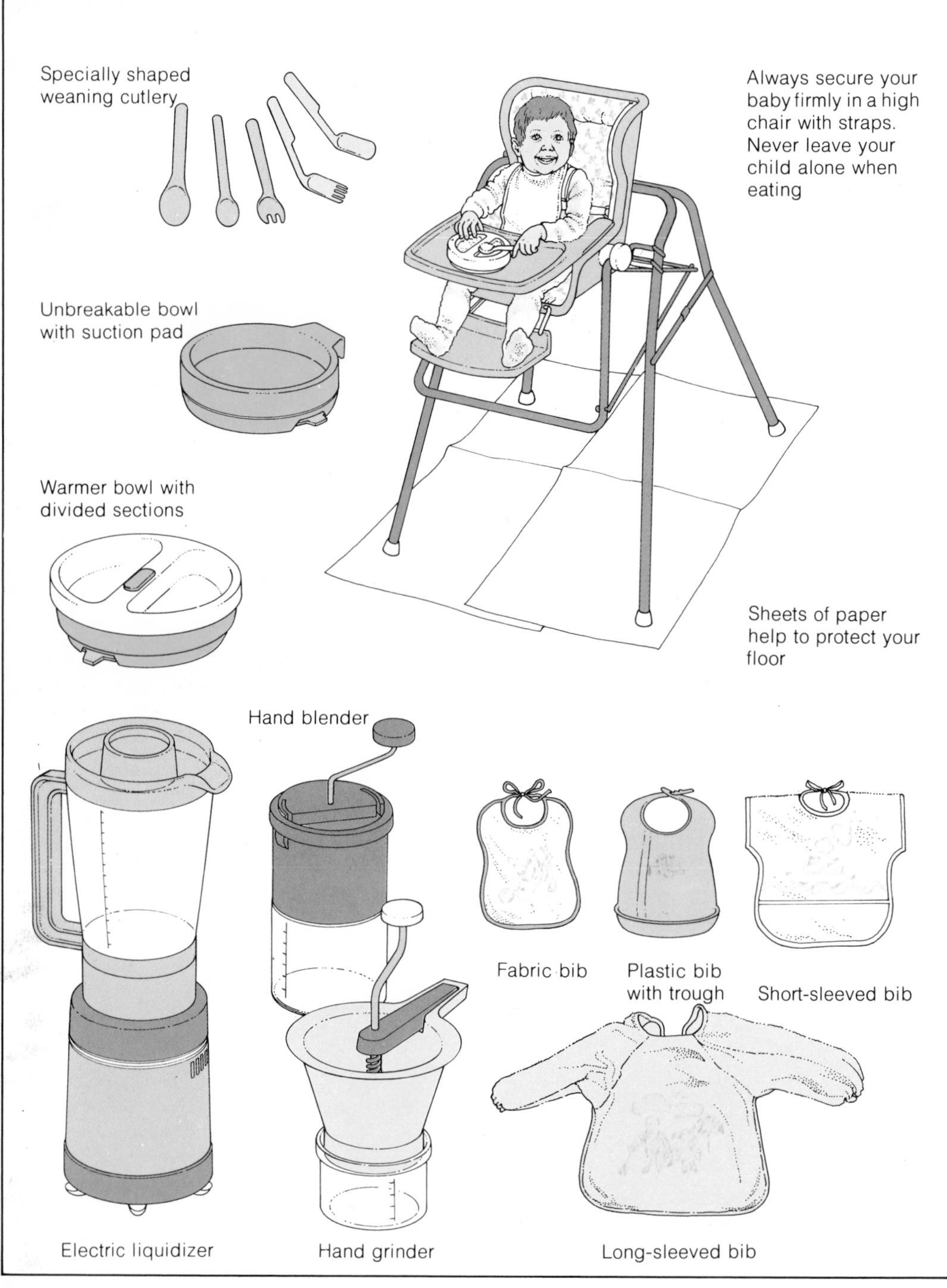

Feeding patterns

By 8 months most babies will probably be eating two or three small meals a day, with an early morning and bedtime breastfeed or bottle. As far as you can, adjust your baby's mealtimes so that they coincide with the rest of the family.

Obviously every family has a different schedule but try and be flexible and, if necessary and possible, alter your normal routine slightly to accommodate the baby. In a few months she will learn to fit into your schedule. If you are alone with the baby all day make sure you have your meals and snacks at the same time as her because it is largely through example that she will learn how to eat properly.

Being part of the family

Pull the baby's highchair up to the table so that she feels she is really participating in an activity that you and the rest of the family are also involved in, rather than simply being a passive recipient of whatever is put in her mouth. Many parents have found that babies who seem to be difficult feeders greatly improve when they eat in company.

Mealtimes can be messy

Inevitably, for the next few months, mealtimes can be messy but try and resign yourself to it rather than hope to control it. Exploring the texture of everything you give her by delving her hands into it and covering it all over the highchair and herself is a crucial part of the learning process. By the time she is a year old you will be surprised at how much physical control over her fingers, spoon and cup she will have developed if she has been encouraged in the early months to participate in feeding herself as much as possible.

The end of breastfeeding

Another advantage of establishing a regular eating pattern for the baby based on the rest of the family's schedule is that it helps mothers who are still breastfeeding to cut out the daytime feeds. Sitting in a high chair puts not only a physical but also a psychological distance between baby and breast and her enjoyment of the family's company usually results in her quickly forgetting to want or expect daytime feeds.

At 10 months

By 10 months the range of foods eaten will have taken over as the main nutrient sources and you will almost certainly find that you can stop breastfeeding altogether, if you wish, by offering an alternative drink. Although your milk supply will have decreased as the baby drops her daytime feeds, you and your baby may still enjoy one breastfeed a day, usually last thing before bed. Some babies derive a great deal of comfort from this and as long as you are happy there is no need to stop until the baby gives up of her own accord.

Start using a teacher beaker at mealtimes

Provided there is sufficient variety in the diet to supply the baby's needs for protein and calcium, there is no need to switch from breast milk to formula feed or to introduce cow's milk at this stage. If used, cow's milk should be boiled and diluted at first because babies who have been breastfed may not appreciate the new taste. By one year cow's milk can be given unboiled and the addition of grain coffee (see page 59) is often liked. The daily intake of milk need not exceed 570 ml (1 pint) from this time on as milk is not a complete food and certain nutrients may be lacking in the diet of a child who drinks milk to the exclusion of other foods. The possibility of a milk intolerance should be investigated if the child is prone to persistent colds, catarrh, sinus problems, sore throats or skin complaints such as eczema. If this is found to be the case milk can be removed completely from the diet and professional advice taken as to the most appropriate alternative.

Vegan babies

Babies of parents who eat no animal produce (vegans) should use a complete milk substitute in place of breast milk when breastfeeding stops. Modified and fortified soya milk formula is available but further supplementation may be required (see Nutrient chart page 16). Ask your doctor or health visitor for advice and consult the Nutrient chart (see page 16) for sources of calcium, protein and vitamin B12. For those wishing to use dairy produce, cow's and goat's milk yoghurt and curd or cottage cheese are generally easier to digest than milk or hard cheeses and yet are still good sources of protein and calcium and, provided whole milk is used, they contain the important fat-soluble vitamins A and D.

Food variety

Between 9 and 12 months when the baby's mealtimes have settled down in to a fairly regular pattern try introducing her to a wide variety of food tastes and textures so that mealtimes are exciting and she does not get into a habit of only eating the same familiar things and rejecting anything new. Most babies are, by instinct, inquisitive and eager to experiment if gently encouraged, so exploit this tendency rather than blunt it. Do not repeatedly give commercially produced baby foods (many of which have a uniformly bland flavour) or the same favourite dishes, day after day. It is tempting if you are in a hurry or the baby is crotchety to give foods which you know she will eat without fuss but this can become counter-productive as the thing she has a passion for one week she may reject the next.

Finger foods

Introduce finger foods as soon as you put your baby in the high chair. They are important for helping with teething and they encourage chewing and biting as opposed to sucking. They are also excellent for keeping little fingers occupied and out of the bowl of puréed food you are trying to feed your baby. Thin strips of raw or cooked vegetable or fruit – carrot, parsnip, cucumber, celery, apple, banana, pear – are all excellent or you can try small lumps of cottage cheese or home-made rusks. Avoid

Finger foods like cooked or raw pieces of fruit and vegetable aid biting and encourage self-feeding

commercial rusks as they contain sugar and wheat. At first, very little will actually be consumed but as the weeks go by and as the teeth appear the baby will get increasingly adept at handling and eating her finger foods. As more teeth emerge she will need more textured meals so put aside a few lumps of cooked vegetable or beans so that she can eat them on her own as well as eating the rest of her meal, mashed, from a spoon. By the time she is a year old it should no longer be necessary even to mash food – she can happily cope with small chopped pieces of meat, fish, vegetables and fruit.

First teeth

There is no set time for the appearance of the first teeth and the number and order of their arrival varies enormously among babies. Some have four or five teeth at 5 months while others still only have that many at 18 months. See diagram below for most common order of appearance.

The milk teeth comprise eight incisors, eight molars and four eye teeth. These should all be present by the third year and it is not until the fifth or sixth year that the second set of teeth begins to appear. What the baby eats during this period is essential to preserve the first teeth and ensure good dietary habits so that the second set can last a lifetime.

FIRST TEETH

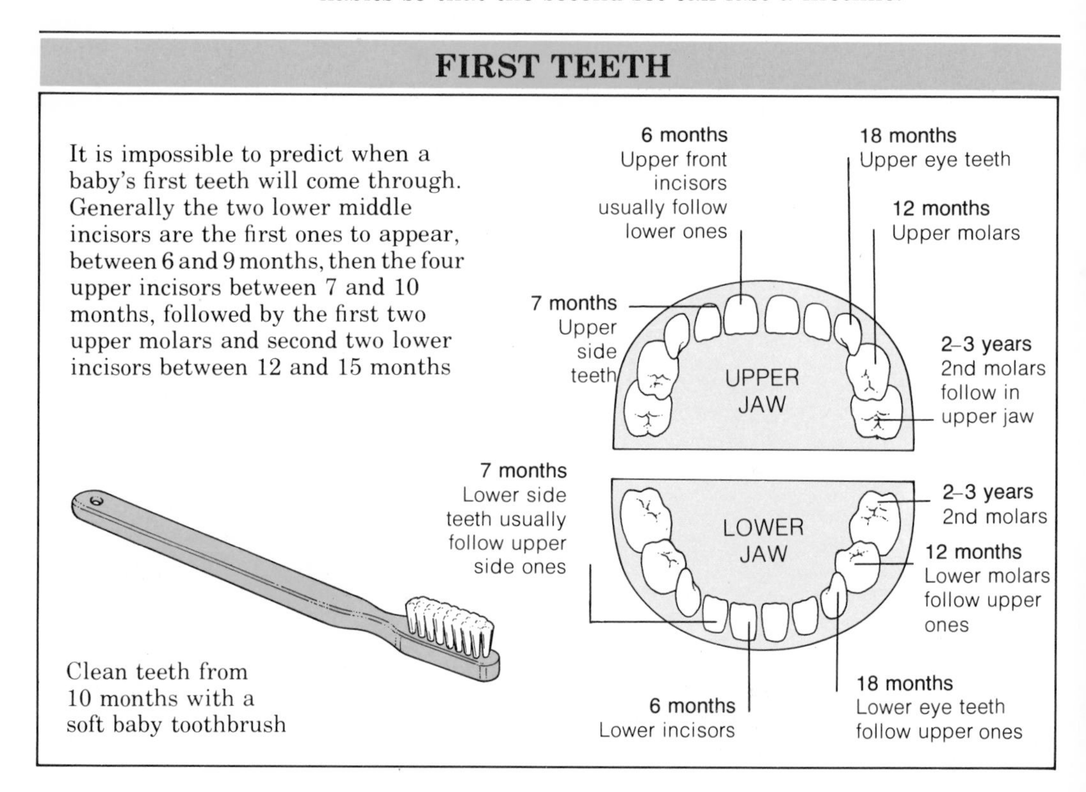

It is impossible to predict when a baby's first teeth will come through. Generally the two lower middle incisors are the first ones to appear, between 6 and 9 months, then the four upper incisors between 7 and 10 months, followed by the first two upper molars and second two lower incisors between 12 and 15 months

Clean teeth from 10 months with a soft baby toothbrush

Teething can irritate the gums but sucking or chewing often seems to help. Giving a sugar-free, salt-free puffed rice cake is far better than a sweet rusk or syrup-filled dummy

Teething

Teething and weaning often occur at about the same time and it can sometimes be difficult to establish whether a stomach upset is due to intolerance of a food or the result of a new tooth appearing. If in doubt remove the food from the diet until teething settles down and try the food again, noting any adverse reaction. Symptoms associated with teething vary but can include loss of appetite, increased temperature, diarrhoea, nappy rash, irritability and painful-sounding crying.

Learning to chew

All children and adults should be encouraged to relax at mealtimes so that they can chew and insalivate their food properly. Chewing aids jaw development (an important prerequisite of speech) as well as stimulating the blood flow that supplies nourishment to the gums and teeth. At the same time it encourages the production of saliva, which contains the enzymes that start the digestion of starch, and protective factors which inhibit the action of bacteria that encourages tooth decay. Avoid drinking during meals as this encourages swallowing unchewed food and is bad for the digestion.

Tooth decay

Many mothers mistakenly believe that syrupy vitamin C drinks are important and essential in the youngest baby's diet and some even go so far as to give them in a feeding bottle or dummy. Prolonged contact of these sticky fluids with the newly forming or formed teeth and the imbalancing effect of refined sugar in the diet combine to hasten both tooth decay and general debility. It has been established that when the body is balanced in minerals the saliva contains factors which protect against bacterial growth in the mouth. Sugar and refined starch upset this natural balance so the health of the teeth will reflect the general health of the body.

Tooth decay is not only the result of exposing the tooth surface to acid-producing sugar but it is also a result of poor nutrition in general.

Fluoride

Adding fluoride to the water supply may delay the process of decay but it does nothing to correct the nutritional imbalances that cause the susceptibility to decay in the first place. In fact there is evidence to suggest that fluoridated water is a potential hazard for those whose health is debilitated as a result of faulty eating. Those at risk include the elderly, people suffering from chronic degenerative diseases and undernourished infants. Where a range of fluoride supplements and toothpastes is available it would seem unwise to resort to mass medication.

Gum disease often causes later tooth loss and again the general cause is faulty nutrition. The breakdown of gum tissue cells and the resulting infection cannot be cured by mouthwashes or toothpastes so the only answer is a better diet.

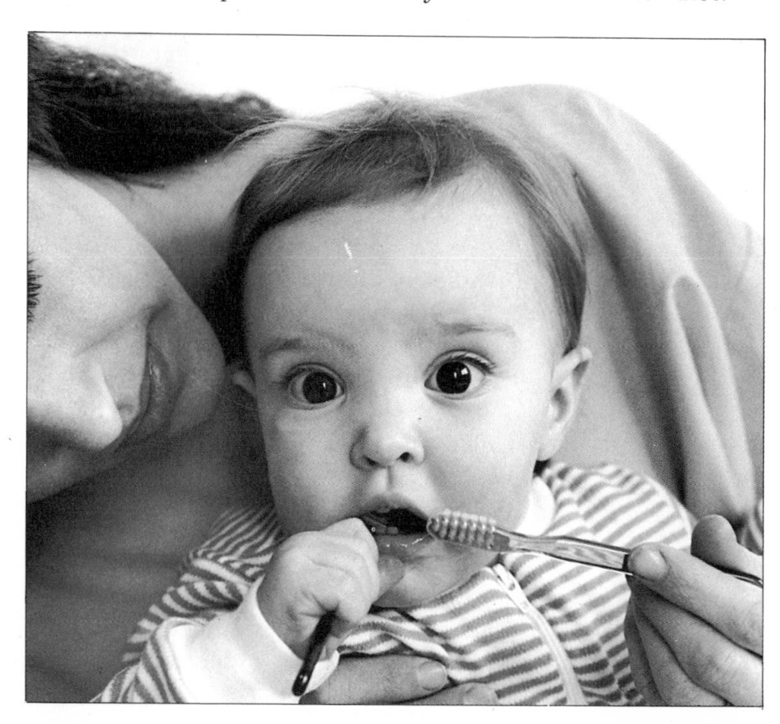

Start cleaning your baby's teeth at about 10 months. At first she will only suck and bite the toothbrush but gradually you can show her how to clean them properly

Common worries during the first year

The process of weaning a baby from milk to solids is one that preoccupies parents for many months. During this time a number of worries and concerns may occur even for the parents of those babies who have an easy and successful transition. There are bound to be occasions when your baby loses her appetite inexplicably or she experiences vomiting or diarrhoea and you will be understandably anxious until you can identify what caused the problem.

The following paragraphs try to pinpoint some of the commonest worries that parents have in the first year and give some advice about how to deal with them.

How much should a baby eat?

The most basic question that concerns parents is – How much should my baby eat? – and unfortunately it is impossible to give an answer that will apply to everyone; every child is different and many have appetites which can change from day to day. At 9 months some babies will eat only half a dozen teaspoonfuls of a cooked dish plus a selection of finger foods at a meal; other babies may eat a complete bowl of stew plus a slice of bread followed by a portion of fruit or yoghurt, before they appear to be satisfied. Be guided by your baby and try to keep mealtimes relaxed and happy occasions so that the baby is not put off her food by your tension.

As amounts being eaten increase, mealtimes can become extended over a considerable time. Slow, steady feeders are the ideal but unfortunately few babies slot into the 'ideal' category. Some enthusiastically consume your painstakingly prepared concoctions with little ceremony whilst others prefer to play with the spoon and have to be coaxed to try even a morsel.

Avoiding excess weight gain

A possible problem with very enthusiastic eaters is that they can become overweight. It is tempting to feed increasingly large portions to a child who is obviously enjoying what you provide but if this is resulting in excessive weight gain it would be better to encourage such a child to feed herself as a practical way of reducing intake to more normal amounts. Overweight children who are offered a free selection of nourishing food tend to eat less when allowed to feed themselves than when spoonfed. Be sure that your baby really is overweight before restricting her intake. Many babies have a plump stage around 9 or 10 months but once they start walking they slim down. Seek your doctor or health visitor's advice if you are worried.

Slow, difficult feeders

Excessively slow eaters often develop this habit because they enjoy the social contact and attention which they get at mealtimes rather than because they dislike the food or are not hungry. It is important with such children to be tolerant and avoid turning mealtimes into a battleground but, on the other hand, a constant round of toys, songs, games and other distracting devices can lead to dining-room chaos and any success gained by these methods is shortlived. Your intelligent infant soon learns just how far you are prepared to go to persuade her to clear her plate. It is far better to try and offer plenty of attention in the form of play and affection outside mealtimes.

Will a baby starve?

Babies are very strong on survival and conditions have to be extreme before they allow themselves to be undernourished when the opportunity is there for them to be well fed. So if they don't want to eat everything on their plate, respect their judgement and try not to prolong mealtimes unnecessarily. It is usually wiser to allow a child to get out of her high chair or down from the table as soon as she has finished eating, rather than forcing her to wait until the rest of the family has finished.

Likes and dislikes

Some babies seem to develop passions for certain foods, such as bananas, milk or eggs, demanding and eating them in alarming quantities. Generally speaking, this is quite normal and providing other nourishing foods are introduced into the diet the current favourite will quickly become just one of a range of preferred dishes. However, if this limited eating trend appears to be more than just a passing phase and continues for more than a few days at the expense of other foods, you may suspect that your baby is not getting a well-balanced diet. Seek advice – it could be that your baby is lacking some important nutrient. Compulsive eating and limited food choice may be an indication of a food allergy where the allergen (the substance causing the symptoms associated with the allergy) becomes an 'essential' in the daily diet. The withdrawal of the food may result in temporary worsening of the symptoms followed by a rapid improvement.

Often far more worrying is the baby who seems to dislike almost everything. This could be caused by a number of factors. First of all, just because you find something delicious it does not follow that your child automatically will. Adult and infant tastes do not always coincide. Secondly, the colour, temperature or texture of the food could be off-putting to your baby or if the food causes bloating, constipation or diarrhoea this could set up an aversion. Thirdly, if the food is too bland and monotonous your baby might start refusing to eat. This can often occur when the baby is about 10 or 11 months old and wants to eat what everyone else is eating.

If a baby persistently refuses to eat consult your doctor.

Refusal to eat or small appetite?

However, it is important to distinguish between a child who is refusing to eat and a child who has a small appetite. Many parents get very worried that their baby is not eating enough but in fact, if they kept a careful list of all that is actually consumed in one day, they might be surprised to find that much more has been eaten than they thought. Furthermore, some babies, like some adults, do have small appetites and do not need to eat as much as their contemporaries – as long as they are happy and healthy there should be no cause for concern.

Other factors can affect appetite too. Emotional upsets such as a sudden change of environment, loss of a friend, parent or pet or parental disharmony can all affect appetite. Imitation is another important factor. If a child sees its parents constantly snacking and never sitting down to a proper meal, she can hardly be expected to have sound eating habits herself.

Snacks

The question of snacks is a difficult one. Some children prefer to eat little and often, and they should not be forced to do otherwise. However, if this is the case, it is probably better to make a little ritual out of each snack by putting on a bib and sitting down with the child. By doing this you will avoid getting into the situation where the child who is not genuinely hungry but is perhaps bored or seeking attention constantly demands between-meal snacks which ruin her appetite for the proper meal.

The test really comes with the food offered. If a child refuses a snack of a piece of fresh or dried fruit or a yoghurt or a slice of wholemeal bread and peanut butter and rejects a glass of plain water and continues to demand a sweet biscuit, or a chocolate or a fizzy drink, then she is not genuinely hungry.

Healthy snacks can provide a useful, nutritious stop-gap between meals; it can sometimes be a long time for an 11 or 12 month old baby to wait from breakfast to lunch or lunch to tea but snacks need to be handled with caution if they are not to turn into a substitute for proper mealtimes.

What if your child dislikes 'good' food

Many parents get very concerned because their baby will not eat the 'right' things or what are traditionally considered 'good' foods. Once again, this is often a situation where the worry is greater than the problem.

Never force a child to eat something she dislikes but try offering it again a month later, cooked differently. You may be surprised to find she will eat it. If not, consult the Nutrient chart (see page 16) for foods which contain the same nutrients. Suggestions for circumventing children's dislikes are dealt with in Chapter 4.

UNYEASTED RICE BREAD

(Makes 4 small or 2 large loaves)

450 g (16 oz) cooked brown rice
570 ml (1 pint) warm water
900 g (2 lbs) organically grown 100% wholewheat flour or a mixture of wholewheat, barley and rye flours
225 g (8 oz) maize meal
225 g (8 oz) millet flour
1 tsp sea salt (after 12 months)

Thoroughly mix all dry ingredients and add water. Knead to a smooth dough and leave in bowl covered with clean cloth in a draught-free place overnight. Pre-heat oven to 150°C (300°F)/Gas 2. Warm bread tins and lightly brush with oil. Divide dough between pans (re-kneading gently to mix after rising) to fill two-thirds of the tin. Make a slit down centre of loaf and bake for 2 hours or until they sound hollow when tapped on the base. This gives a very close textured, chewy bread.

MIXED GRAIN BREAD

(Makes 3 small loaves or 16 rolls)

750 g (1½ lbs) flour
425 ml (15 fl oz) water (blood heat)
pinch sea salt (from 12 months)
15 g (½ oz) fresh or dried yeast
1 tsp unrefined sugar

Combine yeast, sugar and 275 ml (10 fl oz) water. Leave 20 minutes. Combine flour (try a quarter rye and three-quarters organic wholewheat) and salt in bowl and place in low oven to warm. Make a well in the centre of flour and pour in yeast and remainder of water. Mix thoroughly with hands until gradually mixture becomes less sticky. Lightly flour a board and knead dough until smooth in texture when cut with a knife. Place in a bowl and cover with a clean, damp cloth. Leave in a warm place to rise until doubled in size (approximately 2 hours). Re-knead and divide evenly for bread or rolls. Place in lightly oiled tins, cover as before and leave to rise, no more than 40 minutes for loaves or 20 minutes for rolls. Pre-heat oven to 230°C (450°F)/Gas 8 and bake bread for 35 minutes and rolls for 15–20 minutes. When ready bread will sound hollow when tapped on base. Cool out of tins and keep at least 3 days before using.

RUSKS

Simply slice 3–4 day old bread into 2.5 cm (1 in) by 7.5 cm (3 in) rectangles. Place on baking tray in very low oven to dry out for 1 hour by which time rusks will be suitably hardened.

BROWN RICE BREAKFAST DISH

(Serves 1–2)

100 g (4 oz) cooked, short grain brown rice
100 ml (4 fl oz) water or water and juice of soaked dried fruit
Optional ingredients;
sesame, sunflower seed or almond meal
25 g (1 oz) finely grated carrot
25 g (1 oz) fruit purée (apricot, apple, pear)
1 tsp light tahini

Combine ingredients of choice in a saucepan omitting fruit purée if used. The simplest version of this dish is the best for a young baby, adding one new ingredient at a time once these are known to be well tolerated. Stir over medium heat, bring to the boil then reduce heat, cover and simmer for 5 minutes. Tahini gives a creamy texture and flavour. Fruit should only be added if there are no digestive difficulties as improperly digested the result could be flatulence and diarrhoea.

BUCKWHEAT OR SOBA NOODLES

(Serves 4)

These noodles are available wheat-free. Fine in texture, easy to digest and quick to cook they can be used from 9–10 months.

Bring water to boil in pot. You will need approximately 1.5 litres (3 pints) of water for 100–225 g (4–8 oz) noodles. Add noodles either whole or in evenly broken stalks. Choose salt-free variety for babies and young children. Simmer 15–20 minutes then drain and keep liquid for soups and sauces.

Use noodles in a wide variety of pulse, vegetable and meat casseroles in place of wholegrains. Examples □ Aduki beans and carrot with leek □ Aduki bean and onion sauce □ Brown lentil sauce □ Vegetable sauce □ Mixed vegetables with arrowroot and tamari sauce □ Minced chicken and broccoli □ Black-eye beans and lamb with carrot and onion sauce.

SPLIT PEA SOUP

(Serves 6–8)

100 g (4 oz) split peas
450 g (16 oz) onions
1 litre (2 pints) water

Wash and soak split peas for several hours or overnight. Finely slice onions and simmer in half the water in an uncovered pot. Remove the froth that forms round the side of the pot then add peas and remaining water. Cover and simmer 30–40 minutes until tender. Sieve to make a thick purée and serve unseasoned or, for an older child, add a taste of yeast extract, sea salt, miso or vegetable stock.

CHICKEN SOUP

(Serves 6–8)

1 chicken carcass plus giblets
1 litre (2 pints) water
150 g (6 oz) onion, quartered
100 g (4 oz) carrot and celery tops (optional)

Place bones, giblets, vegetables and water in a large saucepan and simmer for 1–2 hours. Cool quickly off the heat then strain and use as a basis for a clear soup or thick broth. Keep stock in refrigerator and use within 2–3 days. Re-heat thoroughly before serving.

FISH SOUP

(Serves 6–8)

225 g (8 oz) boneless fish (if using a fish which has bones and skin such as herring or trout, remove these and simmer separately in 275 ml (10 fl oz) water for 20 minutes)
450 g (1 lb) mixed, peeled vegetables (leek, onion, fennel, carrot, cucumber)
1 litre (2 pints) water (including fish stock if available)
pinch sea salt
pinch dill seed (optional)

Dice vegetables and simmer in water for 20–30 minutes until tender. Add dill seed and fish cut into 2.5 cm (1 in) cubes and simmer gently for another 10 minutes or until cooked.

The strained broth is particularly appealing when appetite is poor and the addition of fennel and/or dill seed aids the digestion of fish.

FAMILY FAVOURITE GRAIN BAKE

(Serves 4–6)

100 g (4 oz) short grain brown rice
50 g (2 oz) millet
350 ml (12 fl oz) water
350 g (12 oz) cooked, mashed pumpkin
175 ml (6 oz) dulse stock
150 g (6 oz) grated carrot
100 g (4 oz) leek or onion, finely sliced
100 g (4 oz) cauliflower sprigs
100 g (4 oz) Brussels sprouts, sliced
100 g (4 oz) celery, finely sliced
15 g (½ oz) fresh herbs, finely chopped

Cook rice and millet in water for 40 minutes then mix well with vegetables, stock and herbs. Put into ovenproof casserole, cover and bake for 40 minutes at 180°C (350°F)/Gas 4 or steam for 1 hour.

Variations □ 50 g (2 oz) sunflower seeds can be cooked with the grain or toasted and added with the vegetables or added as a topping before serving □ 175 g (6 oz) cooked beans or lentils can be added with the vegetables to give a complete meal in one dish. Serve with seasonal salad □ 1 whole egg or 2 egg yolks can be added to mixture before baking.

LENTIL OR LITTLE BEAN STEW

(From 8 months. Serves 4–6)

50 g (2 oz) whole lentils (mung beans, aduki beans or yellow mung dahl)
100 g (4 oz) carrot, parsnip, turnip or swede, diced
50 g (2 oz) brown rice, millet, barley or oatflakes or cooked brown rice
425 ml (15 fl oz) kombu stock
pinch dried herbs (optional)

Soak, then carefully wash lentils checking for tiny stones. Put in pot with stock and bring to the boil. Add vegetables, herbs (dill or caraway seed aid digestion) and rice flakes and cook gently until beans are soft (see page 122 for cooking times). The mixture should resemble a thick soup. Sieve or liquidize at first. Adapt for older babies by serving unsieved and using larger beans. Always boil beans for at least 10 minutes before proceeding with gentler cooking. Later a strip of kombu seaweed can also be added to aid digestion and add minerals.

Serve with additional seasonal vegetables.

GRAIN AND BEAN PURÉE

(From 8 months. Serves 4)

50 g (2 oz) short grain brown rice
570 ml (1 pint) water or vegetable stock
25 g (1 oz) oatgroats (optional)
15 g (½ oz) sunflower seeds, toasted and finely ground
15 g (½ oz) aduki beans

Lightly dry roast the rice in a heavy pot. Add seeds, beans and water. Bring to boil and simmer 50–60 minutes until grains and beans are soft. Sieve through a muslin at first then gradually serve more textured. Serve warm or cold.

Variations □ In place of rice use millet or barley □ In place of sunflower seeds use ground pumpkin seeds, sesame seeds, almonds or cashews □ In place of aduki beans use green lentils, red lentils, mung beans or split peas.

BABY NUTROAST

(From 9 months. Serves 4)

25 g (1 oz) sunflower seeds, finely ground and lightly toasted
25 g (1 oz) sweet almonds, finely ground
100 g (4 oz) carrot, grated
100 g (4 oz) cooked brown rice

Combine all ingredients and mix well. Press mixture into small loaf tin or divide into small patties and bake at 140°C (300°F)/Gas 4 for 20 minutes. Alternatively, add a little hot water to bind, place in a bowl, cover and steam 20–30 minutes. Serve hot or cold.

BARLEY CASSEROLE

(From 8 months. Serves 4)

275 ml (½ pint) kombu stock or water
50 g (2 oz) carrot or carrot and turnip, finely grated
50 g (2 oz) cooked split peas or whole lentils
25 g (1 oz) barley
25 g (1 oz) scallions/spring onions, sliced

Dry roast barley in heavy pot until golden and put in ovenproof casserole. Add vegetables and pulses, cover with stock and casserole lid. Bake at 180°C (350°F)/Gas 5 for 1 hour. Sieve for young babies.

This dish can also be made as a stew.

STEAMED FISH

(Serves 2–3)

100–150 g (4–6 oz) fillet of fish (haddock, whiting, sole)
½ tsp oil
1 tsp freshly squeezed lemon juice
pinch sea salt (optional)

Brush heatproof soup or dinner plate with oil. Place fish on plate and season if appropriate. Cover with a piece of greaseproof paper, set over a pan of boiling water and cover with pot lid. Keep water boiling and cook 15–20 minutes until fish is moist and tender. Check for bones before serving (see Kedgeree recipe page 85) or use in fish salad or with sauce as in Poached fish (see page 68)

CHICKEN PIE

(Serves 4)

225 g (8 oz) roast chicken
75 g (3 oz) each of onion, leek, carrot, turnip
50 g (2 oz) walnuts (optional)
350 g (12 oz) cooked, mashed potato
175 ml (6 fl oz) stock from chicken

Cook onion until tender in enough stock to cover. Add remaining vegetables and cook a further 10 minutes. Add walnuts, chicken and sufficient stock to moisten then turn into ovenproof casserole and top with potatoes. Bake in pre-heated oven at 180°C (350°F)/Gas 4 for 30–40 minutes. Serve with lightly steamed greens or salad.

SCALLOPED POTATOES

(Serves 4–6)

450 g (1 lb) each potato and onion
175–225 ml (6–8 fl oz) stock
225 g (8 oz) cooked lentils (optional)
225 g (8 oz) roughly grated carrot
100 g (4 oz) toasted flaked almonds

Slice onion and potato very thinly. Put beans, if used, in base of ovenproof dish and top with layers of vegetables. Barely cover with stock and bake with a lid on for 1 hour at 180°C (350°F)/Gas 4 then uncovered for 30 minutes at 170°C (325°F)/Gas 3. Serve sprinkled with nuts and with lightly steamed greens.

LIVER SLIVERS

(Serves 2–3)

100 g (4 oz) liver (chicken or lamb is milder than pig or calf)
25 g (1 oz) brown rice or barley flour
pinch dried thyme (optional)
pinch sea salt (optional)
25 g (1 oz) oil
100 g (4 oz) onion or leek, finely sliced
25 g (1 oz) mushrooms (optional)

Wipe liver and slice into 5 cm (2 in) strips or slivers. Soak in milk for 1–2 hours to remove any strong flavour if necessary. Meanwhile heat half the oil in shallow pot and add onion or leek cooking gently until soft. Toss liver in flour, herb and salt mixture and add to pot with onions and remaining oil if required. Add mushrooms, either sliced if large or whole if small. When outside of liver is browned and juices extracted from mushrooms, cover, turn down heat and cook gently a further 5–10 minutes until liver is tender but not dry.

Serve as a purée for a young child, or as a spread on toast or on a bed of brown rice, millet or potato with a crunchy finger salad for older children. Give a fresh orange or mandarin for dessert so that the vitamin C from the fruit can aid the absorption of iron from the liver.

CAULIFLOWER SUPREME

(Serves 4–6)

450 g (1 lb) cauliflower
225 g (8 oz) onion, very finely sliced
450 g (1 lb) cooked millet
25 g (1 oz) oil (optional)
50 g (2 oz) light tahini
50 g (2 oz) fine breadcrumbs
25 g (1 oz) sunflower or sesame seed meal

Steam then mash cauliflower. Add millet and, if required to moisten, stock from cauliflower. Gently shallow fry or simmer onion until soft. Add to millet with tahini. Put in ovenproof casserole, top with breadcrumbs and seed meal or layer cauliflower and millet mixed with onion and tahini. Bake for 30–40 minutes at 180°C (350°F)/Gas 4.

Alternatively a little finely grated feta cheese can be added to the topping or 150 g (6 oz) cooked beans or lentils can be added to millet mix.

VEGETABLES

(Low water cooking. Serves 3–4)

15 cm (6 in) strip kombu seaweed
75 g (3 oz) each of the following combination of vegetables – carrot, turnip, Brussels sprouts or pumpkin, onion and cauliflower or leek, carrot and broccoli or Chinese leaves, spring onion bulbs and swede or selection of choice from seasonal fresh produce
175 ml (6 fl oz) water

Soak kombu in water for 2–3 minutes until soft. Reserve soaking water. Slice kombu into 2.5 cm (1 in) strips and use to line bottom of a pot with a tight-fitting lid. Prepare vegetables and slice according to type. Choose slicing method that will ensure even cooking of all vegetables. Arrange in layers on top of kombu making the quickest cooked vegetable the top layer. Add kombu water and then cover pot. Bring to boil and simmer for 10–15 minutes. If lid is not tight fitting you may need to add a little more water.

Use any remaining liquid as a mineral-rich drink. Dilute and serve warm or cold or add to soups. Serve with crunchy bean sprouts for older children.

VEGETABLE SAUCE

(Serves 4–6)

15 cm (6 in) strip kombu seaweed or wakame or dulse
225 g (8 oz) pumpkin
225 g (8 oz) carrot
275 ml (½ pint) water

Soak seaweed of choice in a little water for 2 minutes to soften then cut into 2.5 cm (1 in) strips and place on bottom of heavy pot. Layer slices of pumpkin and carrot on top of this adding just enough water to cover. Put lid on pot, bring to the boil and simmer for 20 minutes until vegetables are tender. Sieve and dilute as required to make a smooth sauce. Serve over lightly cooked cauliflower or with cooked grain and pulse dishes.

The addition of a ¼ tsp of brown rice syrup, barley malt or molasses to a bean or vegetable dish can encourage the most stubborn disliker of savoury foods to try these delicacies. It is better to do this than bribing with a dessert or sweets.

YOGHURT

(From 9 months. Serves 4)

570 ml (1 pint) milk
1–2 tsp natural yoghurt
1 wide-necked flask and a cooking thermometer (range 37°–100°C/100°–212°F)

Heat milk to 81°C (180°F) but do not boil. Allow to cool to between 42°–48°C (110°–120°F). Put yoghurt in flask and gently stir in milk. Seal flask and leave for 3–6 hours in a warm place to set, then store in refrigerator for 2–3 days. Reserve a little for next batch starter. Flask should be washed and sterilized between each batch.

CURD CHEESE

(Serves 4)

Warm 1 pint of milk to blood heat. Place a dessertspoonful of natural yoghurt in a wide-necked flask, add milk, stir gently to mix. Seal and keep in warm place until milk is set (3–6 hours). Pour into a muslin bag and suspend over a basin for 12 hours. The whey drains out of the milk leaving lumpy curds. To make a smooth cheese add a little fresh cream or milk and blend with a handwhisk. Freshly chopped herbs are a delicious addition.

REAL CUSTARD

(Serves 2–3)

25 g (1 oz) fine polenta or maize meal
225 ml (8 fl oz) water

Blend ingredients, add to pot and bring to the boil stirring constantly. Flavour with real vanilla essence or vanilla pod. Sweeten delicately with unsweetened apple juice, barley malt or brown rice syrup.

JELLY GLAZE

(Serves 2–3)

275 ml (½ pint) juice of choice
15 g (½ oz) arrowroot or kuzu diluted in a little cold liquid

Stir arrowroot mixture into heated juice and bring to boil. When ready mixture will turn clear. Pour over fruit and leave to set.

POACHED WHOLE FRUITS

(Use 50–100 g [2–4 oz] fruit per serving)

Peaches, pears, apples, plums and apricots make a naturally sweet dessert when poached in a little unsweetened organic apple juice or blackcurrant juice. Place fruit and juice in a pot and simmer for 5 minutes or bake in preheated oven 190°C (375°F)/Gas 5 for 15–20 minutes.

UNSWEETENED FRUIT JUICE JELLIES

(Serves 2–3)

275 ml (½ pint) diluted juice of choice (apple, blackcurrant, pear or red grape)
3 tsp agar agar in flaked or powdered form (more may be required depending on brand)

Bring juice to simmering and stir in agar agar to thicken. Turn into mould to set.

CAROB SAUCE

(From 6–9 months. Serves 1–2)

125 ml (¼ pint) water or milk
1 tsp brown riceflour or arrowroot
1 tsp carob flour

Sieve flour and carob into a bowl. Gradually stir in water to make a smooth paste. Bring the mixture to the boil and serve warm or cold.

TAHINI SAUCE

(From 6–9 months. Serves 1–2)

125 ml (¼ pint) water or milk
1 tsp maize meal or polenta
1 tsp light tahini
2 tbs cold water
vanilla pod

Place the vanilla pod in the water or milk and simmer for 2–3 minutes to release flavour. Meanwhile mix maize meal and tahini in a bowl with 2 tbs cold water. Remove vanilla, bring mixture to the boil and pour over tahini mixture. Stir vigorously to mix, returning to pot to ensure thickening, adding a little extra liquid if required. Cool and serve plain or with stewed fruit.

APRICOT KANTEN

(Serves 2–4)

100 g (4 oz) dried apricots, pre-soaked in 225 ml (8 fl oz) water
15 g (½ oz) arrowroot or kuzu dissolved in a little cold water

Simmer apricots in soaking water until tender. Strain and chop, reserving juice. Make juice up to 225 ml (8 fl oz), re-heat and stir in arrowroot to thicken. Pour over apricots and leave to set or purée apricots and stir into thickened juice. This also makes an attractive dinner party dessert decorated with toasted flaked almonds.

JAPANESE TWIG TEA

Also known as bancha, kukicha or three-year tea, it is made from winter harvested and roasted twigs of the three year old tea bushes. Free from the stimulants caffeine and tannin it is especially beneficial to children because of its high calcium content. Hot or cold it is a refreshing drink, ideal for children who are sensitive to milk and other dairy products. Also recommended for tense parents!

To release the full flavour of the tea, simmer 2 tbs twigs in 570 ml (1 pint) water for 10–20 minutes. Strain and dilute to taste. Serve without milk or sweetener. Left-over tea can be re-heated and twigs can be re-simmered with fresh water. Twig tea is also available as teabags which are useful when travelling.

ROASTED DANDELION ROOT COFFEE

Pieces of roasted dandelion root can be bought in dried form. If home-roasting fresh roots only harvest those especially grown for the purpose. Hedgerows and fields are invariably sprayed with herbicides and pesticides. Busy roadways have high levels of lead in vegetation. Instant varieties contain lactose (milk sugar) which may be unsuitable for some children.

Add 1 tbs roasted root to 570 ml (1 pint) water and simmer for 5–10 minutes for a rich flavoured brew that resembles black coffee. Dilute to taste and flavour with a little barley malt for a warming winter drink.

INSTANT GRAIN COFFEES

A variety of instant, roasted grain drinks are available and the suitability of these will depend on individual tolerance of the grains. Most use barley and chicory which give a mild, pleasantly flavoured warm or cold drink, which is additive- and caffeine-free. Approximately ½ tsp is required per cup.

BARLEY WATER

A refreshing barley water can be made by adding the juice of a freshly strained lemon to barley tea with the optional addition of 1–2 tsp barley malt or honey.

BARLEY TEA

25 g (1 oz) barley
570 ml (1 pint) water

Roast barley in a pot until golden. Cool slightly, add water and simmer for 20–30 minutes – strain and serve hot or cold.

HERBAL TEAS

Herbs make attractive and aromatic plants in a garden or on a windowsill and fresh leaves infused in boiled water give mild flavoured drinks known in France as 'tisane'. These should be used with caution, however, as certain herbs have specific medicinal properties.

Mild herbs such as fennel, lime or chamomile make refreshing drinks for summer use. Freshly harvested leaves can be dried and stored for winter use. Avoid strong infusions for children and be cautious of the overuse of any one variety. Commercially available herb and spice mixtures are not suitable for children.

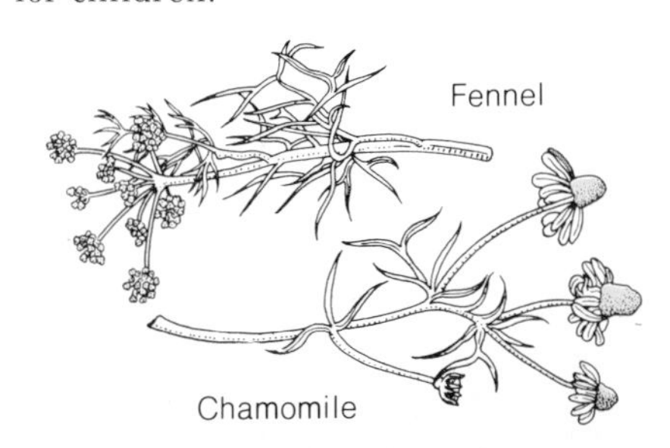

4 From 1 to 2 years

The routine at one year

By the time your baby is one year old some sort of eating routine should be established with the baby joining in family mealtimes as much as possible. It is important for a young child to be present at these meals even if he has already eaten his main meal earlier in the day because they are one of the principal occasions when all or most of the family are present. Undoubtedly, a certain amount of organization is required if both parents are out at work or if there are other children of varying ages demanding food on return from school.

Frequently the older children's after-school snack and the baby's teatime coincide and this provides a good opportunity for the parent to share it with his or her children. A bowl of soup, cereal, a home-made scone or biscuit with a glass of diluted fruit juice is a better snack than a chocolate biscuit or packet of crisps. Most older children enjoy coming home to this 'meal' which can, in fact, be part of the first course of their main meal with the remainder eaten at a later stage, perhaps with both parents, after the baby is in bed. The organization of meals for shift-working parents need not necessarily be a problem as those doing night-shift can eat their 'breakfast' when the children are eating their tea or supper and when they return in the morning they can join their family at the breakfast table.

The importance of mealtimes

Because each child and each family situation is different there can be no set plan for mealtimes other than that they should follow a regular pattern. It is unfair and, in the long run, nutritionally unsound to expect a young child to tolerate either long gaps between meals or a series of hastily prepared snacks and late-night main meals. During times of disrupted routine such as moving house, travelling or crisis it is important that infant feeding times be as regular and orderly as possible to retain some continuity and minimize upset.

It is important, especially as family members grow older, to meet at a mealtime at least once a day, and these should be relaxed and enjoyable occasions, preferably uninterrupted by television and friends calling for children to go out to play. Mealtimes should never become lecture sessions and if there is a behaviour problem this is best sorted out before the meal.

The baby will love having his tea with an older brother or sister who has just come home from school

Avoid conflict or tension at meals

Any pre-meal disagreement between parents should if possible be resolved or at least set aside for the duration of the meal. Children are quick to sense tension and if this is continually associated with mealtimes the long-term effect could be an upset digestion and erratic eating habits. Even in the best of relationships there is an occasional disagreement and as the dinner table is an important meeting place it could easily become the place of conflict. By all means sort out the problem there and then but don't forget to let your children see that you are friends again!

A good, mixed diet

By now your child should be eating a good mixed diet, including plenty of fibre (see Appendix 1, Glossary of foods page 114), and a wide range of foods which are very similar to the rest of the family. There should be no necessity to cook separate meals for the baby as long as you avoid putting salt and highly spiced seasonings into the food at the cooking stage. Older children and adults can add it to their food once it has been served, if they wish. Garlic, onions and herbs are no problem as most babies enjoy the added flavour that they give to stews and casseroles. If the whole family is following the kind of healthy eating pattern outlined in Chapter 1 your baby's diet should, by now, be presenting very few difficulties in terms of cooking or special preparation.

Table manners

The introduction of table manners at this stage is important for you and your child. Unsociable habits such as tantrums, squealing, throwing food and constant attention-seeking may be tolerated as a passing phase but if allowed to take hold as a normal pattern of behaviour will result in you and your child being excluded from social events where eating is involved.

Most children want to be loved and praised by their parents and between one and two years old are perfectly capable of understanding basic table manners as long as parents are firm and consistent in their approach. Do not get genuinely cross or tense with a child who does not obey your instructions immediately. It takes time for them to realize that you mean what you say, every time. A young child is bound to put your authority to the test but if your standards are consistent and you give lots of praise when they are adhered to (and a quick, firm but unmalicious rebuke when they are not) then your child will soon adopt the pattern of behaviour which he knows wins your approval. All teaching and learning should be fun. Do not expect that teaching good eating habits will be a problem. Many children do not have any difficulty in accepting them quite naturally.

If family mealtimes are relaxed and happy occasions there should be no difficulty teaching your child good table manners

Some children who have bad manners at home react quite differently when they are away. A sense of occasion can often bring out the best in us all – eating at friends, in a restaurant or on holiday can often be easier than at home where the routine may have become rather dull and monotonous for your child. Never leave your child on his own during mealtimes because apart from the risk of choking (see page 109) he can also become very bored and lonely. Later in life, the association of these emotions with food could mean consolation eating which in turn could lead to underweight or overweight and diseases related to those conditions such as anorexia nervosa and bulimia nervosa. Similarly, do not use food to keep children quiet. If a child is genuinely hungry between meals make a point of ensuring that the food you are giving is supplying sufficient nutrients and calories. If a meal runs unexpectedly late or something happens which disrupts the routine have available some favourite nibbles such as dried fruits, home-made biscuits, raw vegetables or slices of fruit spread with sunflower spread to keep your child going.

Food fads

Most children go through phases with likes and dislikes which may change from week to week. Within reason these are often best accommodated. There may be an underlying food intolerance which results either in your child avoiding a food or

Not even twins can be expected to have the same food preferences. Food fads come and go but are of little importance in a balanced, wholefood diet

demanding it at every meal. There is no need for concern if your child is thriving, active and otherwise healthy. If the diet fads persist and the food choice is very limited it is important to seek professional advice. Short fasts brought on by lack of appetite can be a natural way for the body to speed up the elimination of an illness, but remember, during a fever it is essential to maintain fluid intake.

Gentle persuasion and involving an older child in the choice and preparation of food can often resolve an eating problem. In most cases it is the parents rather than the child who needs advice. Overfussing can be just as counterproductive as neglect.

Never force a child to eat

Do not force a child to eat any food – you will rarely succeed and only build up fear and resentment. The secret is to establish a liking for wholefoods early in life and to offer a selection of tasty, nourishing foods at mealtimes. An appetite for good foods taken in moderation is to be encouraged. All temptation to introduce between-meal snacks and three-course lunches and dinners should be strongly resisted. The first few years of life will be the only time, in theory at least, when as parents you will be in control of your child's eating habits. Make full use of this time so that whatever deviation your child might make when exposed to school meals, tuck shops and friends' mothers, the balance can be restored, in part at least, at the family meal table.

Subterfuge and disguise

There may be a good reason why a child dislikes a food in which case an alternative food with similar nutritive value should be used. If, however, the dislike is a purely visual or textural one there are a variety of ways in which one can disguise and enrich foods to increase their appeal.

Vegetables

Children who refuse vegetables frequently have parents with a similar dislike. Vegetables are often presented in an unattractive way as an overcooked watery mass and it is no wonder they are disliked. Vegetables as purées and sauces, or steamed and delicately flavoured with natural yoghurt, nut or seed creams, or pulses are more suitable. From around 2 years raw vegetables are often preferred to cooked ones – serve finely grated or as finger foods. Although sugar should generally be avoided adding a taste of brown rice syrup or barley malt to a vegetable dish can make all the difference to its acceptability and is preferable to bribing with a dessert.

Vegetables can be puréed into soups and sauces or raw juices can be diluted as a drink or added to soups or casseroles after they have been removed from the heat. Blanched or raw vegetables cut into attractive shapes such as flowers, fans, wedges or matchsticks make appealing finger foods (see page 121).

Fruit

This is usually well liked and as a result can be used to disguise other foods. Fruit purée can be served as a sauce mixed with yoghurt or thickened with arrowroot, kuzu, or agar agar to make light, easily digested, additive-free jellies. Fresh or dried fruits can be puréed and diluted with bottled waters to serve as drinks in place of squashes or sweetened, fizzy drinks. End meals with a piece of fresh fruit in place of a dessert or make fresh fruit salad, meringue nests, open-topped fruit pies, fruit crumbles – using flaked wholegrain cereals, flaked nuts, seed meal, organic wholegrain flour, muscovado sugar or concentrated, unsweetened apple juice to sweeten.

Meat

Many children have no particular liking for meat, especially red meat, and they can be very efficient at discovering and rejecting the most cunningly hidden traces. Soups made with vegetables and puréed with the addition of meat are sometimes accepted. Meat spreads and cold meats are often better tolerated than hot dishes but make your own spreads from cooked meats to ensure that they are additive free. If you do not eat meat and you do not wish your child to eat meat take care to offer a nourishing alternative. Consult the Nutrient chart (see page 16) and look at the section on Protein complementation in Appendix 2 (see page 117).

Fish

The bland taste of fish is easily disguised. Take care to remove all bones – these have put more people off eating fish than any actual dislike of the food. Herb or cheese flavoured sauces or fish, vegetable and grain dishes are often preferred to plain boiled or grilled fish. Home-made fish cakes and fish fingers are nourishing and the crisp outer coat appeals to older children.

Eggs

Because of the risk of allergy, particularly to egg whites, eggs are generally introduced at a later stage into the diet. They are usually liked but if your child does not enjoy them boiled or scrambled conceal them in sweet and savoury custards, flans or quiches, as omelette strips, in cakes, puddings or milk shakes.

Cheese

Mild flavoured curd or cottage cheeses are generally liked but their flavour can be enhanced with the addition of freshly chopped herbs, cubes of cucumber, chopped walnuts, toasted flaked hazelnuts, diced fruit, cubes of chicken or finely grated hard cheese. Hard cheeses are generally too salty for young children but later a little grated cheese added to a sauce or crumble topping can enhance the appearance and flavour.

Milk

If milk is not liked the same nutrients can be found in cheeses and yoghurt (using whole milk) or milk can be added to soups, sauces, baking, desserts and home-made ice-cream.

Bread and baking

At certain stages when all your child seems to want is bread or biscuits, home-made versions can be enriched by using wholegrain flours (organically grown) or a mixture of flours, nut and seed meals, grated carrot, bean flours (soya bean flour is particularly rich in protein). Wholesome desserts can be made from beans, wholegrains, fruit, nuts, seeds, and dried fruits.

Nuts and seeds

Although sometimes disliked in their whole form, nuts and seeds can be easily ground to a fine meal and used as spreads or added to porridges, casseroles, baking or desserts. Toasting will bring out the flavour but care must be taken to use only fresh nuts and seeds: as they have a high oil content they can easily become rancid if stored too long.

Beans

There is such a wide variety of pulses that there are bound to be one or two which are liked (see page 122 for cooking times). These can be puréed in soups to give a rich flavour or added to meat casseroles. Bean sprouts are just as high in protein and higher in vitamins than dried beans and make good finger foods while high protein tofu (soya bean curd) has a bland flavour which is easily disguised.

SPROUTING SEEDS, BEANS AND GRAINS

Why sprout?

Sprouting is a form of indoor gardening which, in a matter of days, transforms hard, dry, dormant seeds into crunchy, fresh, leafy vegetables, full of flavour, vitamins and protein.

What to sprout?

Be careful to use only those seeds meant for eating and not ones sold for planting which are often chemically treated. Use sunflower seeds, sesame seeds, mustard cress, alfalfa, mung beans, chickpeas, bengal gram, garbanzo beans, green gram, oats and organic wheat. Lentils and soya beans can be sprouted but are best cooked.

How to use

Some seeds and beans contain substances which prevent the proper digestion of protein. This is not a problem if you are using the sprouts listed as garnishes or finger foods, however cooking is advised when using sprouts as a main ingredient. For the most appetizing results stir-fry sprouts for 2–3 minutes in a shallow pot brushed with oil, then add 1 tablespoon water or stock, cover and steam for 10 minutes. Alternatively, use as a colourful garnish in soups, omelettes, salads and sandwiches.

Equipment

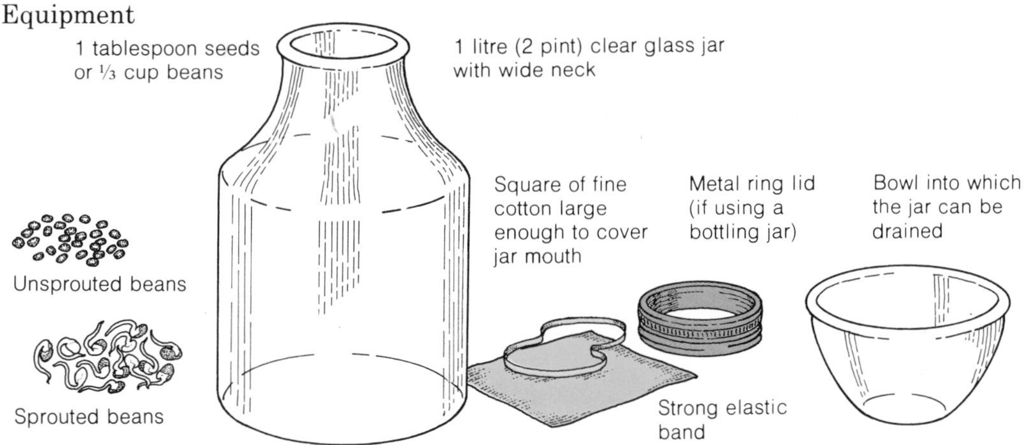

Method

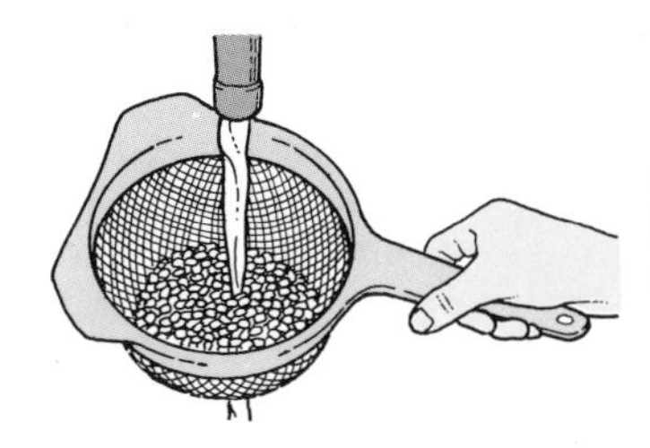

Rinse seeds or beans removing stones, twigs and broken or partial seeds/beans

Place seeds in jar, fill with water and leave to soak overnight
Cover with cotton and drain

Over the following 3 days, rinse and drain twice daily and keep jar in a cool, dark cupboard. To drain properly, tilt the covered end of the jar into a bowl to allow excess moisture to drain out.
Extra rinsing will be required when the weather is warm.
Most beans and seeds will be ready for use in 3–4 days.
Use sprouts fresh or keep in airtight container in refrigerator for 1–2 days

SAVOURY EGG CUSTARD

(Serves 2–4)

2 eggs
275 ml (½ pint) milk
½ tsp yeast extract, dissolved in milk (optional)
1 tsp parsley (optional)

Beat eggs lightly. Warm but do not boil milk and pour over eggs. Strain into lightly oiled ovenproof dish and stand in a tin of water. Top with parsley if used. Bake at 150°C (300°F)/ Gas 1–2 for 1 hour. Test with knife which should come out clean when custard is set.

SAVOURY BREAD AND BUTTER PUDDING

(Serves 3–4)

2 slices organic wholewheat, rye, mixed grain or corn bread, spread with butter
100 g (4 oz) onion or leek, finely sliced
1 egg, beaten
50 g (2 oz) grated mild, white cheese
225 ml (8 fl oz) milk or vegetable stock
¼ tsp yeast extract or pinch sea salt
bayleaf (optional)

Cut bread into 1.25 cm (½ in) cubes and place half in lightly greased ovenproof dish. Cover with half the cheese, then the onion, remaining bread and cheese. If using bayleaf simmer in milk or vegetable stock for 5 minutes then remove and dissolve yeast extract in the liquid. Cool and add to beaten egg. Pour over pudding and bake in pre-heated oven 180°C (350°F)/Gas 4 for 30–40 minutes.

OMELETTE STRIPS

(Serves 2–4)

2 eggs, lightly beaten
1 tbs hot water (boiled and cooled)
2 tsp freshly chopped herbs (parsley, basil, marjoram, savoury, chervil) or
50 g (2 oz) alfalfa sprouts or mung bean sprouts in place of herbs

Combine eggs and water in bowl. Brush a heavy omelette pan with oil and heat. Pour in egg mixture and leave to cook gently until beginning to set. Sprinkle with herbs or sprouts or leave plain. Fold and turn on to plate.

POACHED FISH

(Serves 3–4)

225 g (8 oz) fish fillet
175 ml (6 fl oz) milk or vegetable stock
(bayleaf, pinch sea salt, black pepper, or nutmeg may be used for adults or older children)

Place fillet in pan and cover with milk or stock. Season if appropriate. Bring milk to boil, cover and simmer for 5–8 minutes until fish is tender. This can be checked by separating flesh at the thickest part with a blunt knife. When ready it will flake easily revealing white flesh all the way through. Strain off the milk/stock which can be used to make a sauce.

Carrots, spring onion bulbs and cauliflower sprigs pre-cooked until almost tender make a suitable 'bed' on which to poach fish with a vegetable stock. The vegetables can then be served with the fish and the sauce thickened with arrowroot and flavoured with freshly chopped parsley.

This dish is particularly suitable for babies or children on gluten-free or milk-free diets.

NB Be very careful to remove all bones from fish.

GRILLED FISH

(50–75 g [2–3 oz] per serving)

Depending on type of fish brush with oil on both sides and grill without turning under medium heat. Naturally oily fish such as mackerel, herring and trout can be grilled slit open or closed with pre-cooked vegetable or fruit and herb stuffing. Great care must be taken to remove all bones – check even pre-filleted fish. Fresh or dried herbs can be added to oil or shaken over fish before cooking.

FISH STUFFINGS

Combine ingredients to your own taste as in the following mixtures □ Finely grated carrot, spring onion or chives and toasted flaked ground almonds □ Oatmeal and toasted, ground sesame seeds mixed with vegetable or fish stock with fresh or dried herbs □ Purée of prunes and sesame seed meal □ Freshly grated apple and carrot and finely sliced celery □ Banana slices and freshly pressed orange juice.

SARDINE CRISP

(Serves 2–4)

1 tin sardines in pure olive oil (avoid those in edible oil)
1 tbs freshly squeezed lemon juice
1 ripe tomato (optional)
1 tsp freshly chopped parsley
5 cm (2 in) finely sliced celery or 2.5 cm (1 in) finely sliced cucumber (to garnish)
2 pieces rye crispbread or puffed rice cakes

Drain sardines on kitchen paper to remove excess oil. Mash, including the fine soft bones, then add lemon juice and parsley. Tomato may be pulped and mixed in or sliced and used as decoration. Spread mixture on crispbread.

CHICKEN CHEESE BAKE

(Serves 2)

150 g (6 oz) potato, boiled and mashed
25 g (1 oz) cooked chicken, diced or minced
25 g (1 oz) white cheese, grated
1 ripe diced tomato (skinned and pipped)

Lightly grease a small ovenproof dish. Mix chicken and tomato and place in dish. Combine potato and cheese and spread on top of chicken. Bake at 160°C (325°F)/Gas 3 for 10–15 minutes. An egg added to the potato and cheese makes a more substantial dish.

KIDNEY ON TOAST

(Serves 1–2)

1 lamb's kidney, skinned and cored
15 g (½ oz) butter
50 g (2 oz) leek, finely sliced
25 g (1 oz) cucumber, diced
1 tsp freshly squeezed lemon juice
½ tsp tamari/shoyu soya sauce
50 g (2 oz) finely grated carrot
15 g (½ oz) soaked sultanas
1 slice organic wholewheat or rye toast

Cut kidney into 8 pieces. Heat butter in pan, add leek and cook for 2–3 minutes until soft. Add cucumber and kidney and stir over medium heat until browned. Add soya sauce and cook a further 5–6 minutes. Remove from heat and stir in lemon juice. Cover toast with kidney mixture and top with carrot and sultanas.

SWEET AND SOUR LIVER

(Serves 2–3)

100 g (4 oz) sweet eating apple
100 g (4 oz) onion, in slices or rings
150 g (6 oz) liver (chicken or lamb)
25 ml (1 fl oz) oil
40 g (1½ oz) yoghurt
pinch sea salt (optional)
pinch mixed dried herbs (optional)
50 ml (2 fl oz) water, vegetable, bean or chicken stock

Cook onion rings gently in oil in a heavy, shallow pan until softened. Remove and drain to remove excess oil. Slice liver into 2.5 cm (1 in) strips and toss in same pot until browned on the outside. Remove while the onions are returned to the pot. Top with apple cut into rings or slices and cover with liver. Sprinkle with herbs and salt and gently add stock. Cover pot and cook over lowest heat for 15–20 minutes until liver is tender. Stir in yoghurt and serve with brown rice or potato and leafy salad garnished with grated carrot.

GRAIN AND BEAN LOAVES

(Serves 6–8)

A large variety of savoury main course dishes can be made by adding cooked grains and cooked pulses to vegetables. Combine all ingredients with a well-flavoured stock to make a moist mix and steam for 40–60 minutes or bake for 40 minutes at 180°C (350°F)/Gas 4.

Try the following combinations:

300 g (10 oz) lentils
150 g (6 oz) millet
100 g (4 oz) each leek, carrot, turnip

100 g (4 oz) aduki beans
350 g (12 oz) short grain brown rice
225 g (8 oz) cauliflower

225 g (8 oz) brown lentils
225 g (8 oz) oat or barley flakes
100 g (4 oz) sweetcorn kernels

150 g (6 oz) butter beans
150 g (6 oz) buckwheat
100 g (4 oz) short grain brown rice
100 g (4 oz) each Brussels sprouts, onion

CHRISTMAS CASSEROLE

(From 10 months. Serves 4–6)

225 g (8 oz) Brussels sprouts, quartered
100 g (4 oz) cooked brown rice
75 g (3 oz) cooked chickpeas
100 ml (4 fl oz) chickpea stock
100 g (4 oz) carrot, diced
50 g (2 oz) leek
15 g (½ oz) freshly chopped parsley

Combine cooked chickpeas, brown rice and vegetables and cover with stock and, if required, a little extra water. Simmer for 20 minutes until vegetables are tender then serve with a dessertspoonful of chestnut purée and crunchy alfalfa sprouts.

BUTTERBEAN PURÉE AND SAVOURY MILLET

(Serves 4)

100 g (4 oz) cooked butter beans
100 ml (4 fl oz) bean stock
75 g (3 oz) millet
100 g (4 oz) leek, finely sliced
75 g (3 oz) cauliflower sprigs
75 g (3 oz) carrot, diced
25 g (1 oz) light tahini (optional)
pinch sea salt (optional)
250 ml (9 fl oz) water

Combine millet, water, vegetables and salt in pot. Cover, bring to boil and simmer for 25 minutes. Stir in tahini and turn into ovenproof dish. Purée beans in bean stock and use to cover millet. Heat through in pot if serving immediately or re-heat in oven for 20 minutes at 180°C (350°F)/Gas 4 if using later. Serve garnished with parsley.

TOFU RICE SAVOURY

(Serves 4)

100 g (4 oz) brown rice
350 ml (12 fl oz) water
12 ml (½ fl oz) oil
50 g (2 oz) each, onion or leek, carrot, celery or broccoli, cauliflower or Brussels sprouts, all finely sliced
100 g (4 oz) tofu (add more if wished)
1–2 tsp tamari soya sauce (optional)

Combine rice and water and cook gently for 40–45 minutes. During this time, brush pot with oil and add onion. When soft stir in remaining vegetables and cook for 5 minutes. Add diced tofu and mix well with vegetables. Cook for 3 minutes, add tamari, then mix with rice in pot. Remove from heat, cover and leave for 5–10 minutes to combine flavours. Alternatively, serve rice and vegetables separately.

SCRAMBLED TOFU AND RICE

(Serves 2–4)

100 g (4 oz) cooked brown rice
50 g (2 oz) each, leek, peeled cucumber, sliced and diced
50 g (2 oz) carrot, roughly grated
1 egg
100 g (4 oz) tofu, diced
1–2 tsp tamari soya sauce (optional)
pinch herbs (optional)
1–2 tsp oil

Heat pot and brush with oil. Add leek, cook until tender, then stir in carrot and cook a further 3 minutes. Add tofu, mix well to heat through, then add cucumber. Beat egg to mix, season and add to vegetables in pot, cover and remove from heat. Serve with hot rice or allow to cool and serve sliced in place of sandwiches, with salad.

SALAD INGREDIENTS

Raw lettuces (home-grown are best), radish, celery, beetroot, carrot, Chinese leaves, watercress, mustard cress, cucumber, bean and seed sprouts, alfalfa, mung, triticale, blanched cauliflower and broccoli sprigs, sweet corn – fresh herbs: basil, chives, thyme, marjoram, parsley, dill, fennel, salad onions.

COLESLAW SALAD

(Serves 4)

100 g (4 oz) very finely shredded white cabbage
1 spring onion, very finely sliced (optional)
½ crisp apple (peel, grate or dice just before use)
15 g (½ oz) soaked sultanas (optional)
pinch fennel or caraway seeds (optional)
12 ml (½ fl oz) unsweetened organic apple juice or use carrot juice if not using apple
50 g (2 oz) natural yoghurt, goat or cow's milk (optional)

Combine all ingredients thoroughly and serve. This mixture will store for 1–2 days in refrigerator but is best used fresh. In place of apple and sultanas try shredded dulse. A small, finely grated carrot adds extra colour and taste.

CARROT AND BEETROOT

(Serves 4–6)

100 g (4 oz) finely grated carrot
100 g (4 oz) finely grated raw beetroot
25 g (1 oz) finely sliced peeled celery
25 g (1 oz) soaked sultanas (optional)
25 ml (1 fl oz) unsweetened organic apple juice or organic lacto-fermented carrot or beetroot juice
dash lemon juice (optional)

Combine vegetable ingredients and moisten with juice of choice.

BLACKCURRANT JELLY SALAD

(Serves 2–4)

50 g (2 oz) finely grated carrot
25 g (1 oz) finely grated beetroot
5 cm (2 in) piece celery, finely slope cut
125 ml (¼ pint) unsweetened blackcurrant juice or red grape juice (diluted to taste)
1 tbs freshly pressed lemon juice
2 tsp agar agar powder

Put juice in pot and bring to simmering, stirring in agar agar to thicken. Pour mixture over carrot and beetroot moistened with lemon juice. Jelly can be set in a dampened mould lined with celery or when set shredded with a fork and piled into tiny crisp lettuce leaves.

Alternatively, make a lime jelly salad.

ARAME AND CARROTS

(Serves 4)

25 g (1 oz) arame
150 g (6 oz) leek or onion, finely sliced
100 g (4 oz) carrot matchsticks
1–2 tsp tamari/shoya sauce

Soak arame, in enough water to cover, for 4 minutes. Simmer leek or onion in water for 5 minutes, then add carrot and arame plus soaking water. Cover and simmer for 20 minutes. Add tamari/shoyu sauce and cook a further 5 minutes. Serve hot or cold.

SUMMER CORNBREAD

(Makes 1 loaf)

225 g (8 oz) maize meal
150 g (6 oz) organic whole wheat or barley flour or a mixture of both
pinch sea salt
75 g (3 oz) oil
1 egg beaten with 225 ml (8 fl oz) water or milk
2–4 tbs brown rice syrup or honey
pinch cinnamon (optional)

Pre-heat oven to 220°C (425°F)/Gas 7. Sieve all dry ingredients into a large bowl. Combine egg mixture with honey and oil, then add dry ingredients and stir thoroughly. Lightly oil a 20 cm (8 in) loaf tin, pour in mixture and bake for 20–25 minutes. You may need to cover the bread with a sheet of paper in the last 5 minutes to prevent burning.

INDIAN FLAT BREAD

(Makes 6–8 rounds)

100 g (4 oz) soya flour
50 g (2 oz) maize meal
(or 150 g (6 oz) any flour mix)
150 ml (6 fl oz) water
25 ml (1 fl oz) oil
25 ml (1 fl oz) brown rice syrup (optional)

Combine all ingredients and mix to a smooth batter. Heat a small, heavy pot over medium heat and brush with oil. Pour in half a cup of batter to cover base of pan, then when bubbles burst turn and cook other side.

Keep bread warm by layering beneath a clean tea-cloth.

BASIC BISCUITS

(Makes 15–20)

150 g (6 oz) mixed bean flours
75 g (3 oz) oil
50–75 ml (2–3 fl oz) water
25 g (1 oz) sesame seed meal (optional)
2 tsp baking powder (optional)

Mix all ingredients thoroughly. Drop in dessertspoonfuls on to a lightly greased baking sheet. Bake for 15 minutes at 170°C (325°F)/Gas 3.

HIGH PROTEIN BISCUITS

(Makes 24)

100 g (4 oz) soya flour
50 g (2 oz) bean flour (lima, gram)
75 ml (3 fl oz) oil
25 ml (1 fl oz) barley malt
25 g (1 oz) ground almonds
pinch cinnamon

Cream oil, barley malt and cinnamon. Gradually add flour and almonds to form a smooth dough. Roll into a log shape and cut into 24 pieces. Flatten and bake for 10 minutes at 170°C (325°F)/Gas 3.

REMINISCENT GINGER CRISPS

(Makes 30)

100 g (4 oz) soya flour
50 g (2 oz) brown rice flour
40 g (1½ oz) bean flour
25 ml (1 fl oz) blackstrap molasses
12 ml (½ fl oz) brown rice syrup
50 ml (2 fl oz) boiling water
75 ml (3 fl oz) oil
2 tsp dried ginger
1 tsp each cinnamon and cloves

Gently melt oil, syrup, molasses and water. Pour over mixed flours and flavourings to make a stiff dough. Roll into a log shape and cut into 30 pieces. Flatten and bake for 10 minutes at 170°C (325°F)/Gas 3.

These fill the kitchen with a warm glow and appetizing smell which will bring back memories for years to come!

NB Molasses has laxative properties.

NUT CRISPS

(Makes 25)

50 g (2 oz) maize meal
50 g (2 oz) cashew nuts or blanched almonds
50 g (2 oz) shredded coconut
40 g (1½ oz) soya flour
25 g (1 oz) brown rice flour
40 ml (1½ fl oz) brown rice syrup
50 ml (2 fl oz) oil
50 ml (2 fl oz) water
½ tsp real vanilla essence

Combine dry ingredients in a bowl. Gently warm syrup, oil and water, then remove from heat, add vanilla and pour into centre of bowl. Mix thoroughly. Drop in dessertspoonfuls on to lightly oiled baking sheet. Bake for 20–25 minutes at 180°C (350°F)/Gas 4.

SESAME CRUNCHIES

(Makes 24)

75 g (3 oz) soya flour
75 g (3 oz) sesame seeds
40 g (1½ oz) bean flour
50 ml (2 fl oz) water
40 ml (1½ fl oz) brown rice syrup
40 ml (1½ fl oz) oil

Blend syrup, oil and water, add to remaining ingredients and mix well. Drop in dessertspoonfuls on to an oiled baking sheet and bake for 10–15 minutes at 170°C (325°F)/Gas 3.

JAPANESE ALMOND BISCUITS

(Makes 30)

100 g (4 oz) soya flour
50 g (2 oz) brown rice flour
40 g (1½ oz) bean flour or ground almonds
40 ml (1½ fl oz) brown rice syrup
75 ml (3 fl oz) water
50 ml (2 fl oz) oil
1 tsp real almond essence
15 g (½ oz) flaked almonds

Blend oil, syrup, water and essence. Combine flours and gradually add liquid to make a smooth dough. Roll into walnut-sized rounds, flatten on to lightly oiled baking sheet and press a flaked almond into each biscuit. Bake for 15–20 minutes at 170°C (325°F)/Gas 3.

RICH BROWN RICE PUDDING

(Serves 4)

275 ml (10 fl oz) cow's milk or soya milk
225 g (8 oz) cooked short grain brown rice
40 g (1½ oz) raisins, sultanas or dates
15 g (½ oz) muscovado sugar or honey (optional)

Pre-heat oven to 180°C (350°F)/Gas 4. Heat milk and sugar and pour over rice and dried fruit in an ovenproof dish. Bake for 30–50 minutes at 180°C (350°F)/Gas 4 then for a further 30 minutes at 150°C (300°F)/Gas 2. Serve hot or cold.

TOFU RICE DESSERT

(Serves 4)

150 g (6 oz) tofu
100 g (4 oz) cooked brown rice
100 ml (4 fl oz) milk (dairy or soya)
25 ml (1 fl oz) brown rice syrup
25 g (1 oz) raisins or other dried fruit

Pre-heat oven to 180°C (350°F)/Gas 4. Combine all ingredients and mix thoroughly. Place in lightly oiled ovenproof dish and bake for 25–30 minutes or until set.

TOFU CAROB CUSTARD

(Serves 4)

350 g (12 oz) tofu
1 egg
50 ml (2 fl oz) brown rice syrup
½ tsp real vanilla essence
25 g (1 oz) carob powder

Combine all ingredients in blender until smooth. Place in steaming bowl, cover and steam gently for 10–15 minutes or until just set. Alternatively, divide into small moulds, place them in a pan of water and bake for 15–20 minutes at 170°C (325°F)/Gas 3.

APRICOT ICE-CREAM

(Serves 8)

225 g (8 oz) dried apricots, pre-soaked
225 g (8 oz) vanilla ice cream

Blend and serve as topping over fresh pears.

SUMMERTIME LIME DRINK

50 ml (2 fl oz) freshly squeezed lime juice
350 ml (12 fl oz) bottled water
1 tsp honey or apple juice concentrate

Blend and serve with a sprig of crushed mint.

SPICED APPLE DRINK

350 ml (12 fl oz) unsweetened apple juice diluted with water to taste
5 cm (2 in) cinnamon stick

Simmer juice with cinnamon for 5–10 minutes. Strain and serve warm as a winter treat.

CAROB SHAKE

350 ml (12 fl oz) soya milk
50 g (2 oz) carob powder

Blend and serve.

HOT CHOCOLATE CAROB STYLE

175 ml (6 fl oz) milk
175 ml (6 fl oz) boiling water
50 g (2 oz) carob powder
1 tsp vanilla essence

Blend carob, milk and vanilla then stir in water.

BLACKCURRANT AND APPLE JUICE

175 ml (6 fl oz) water
25 ml (1 fl oz) concentrated unsweetened blackcurrant and apple juice

Use boiling or cold water to dilute juice.

APPLE TWIG TEA

75 ml (3 fl oz) unsweetened apple juice or 25 ml (1 fl oz) concentrate
175 ml (6 fl oz) mild infusion twig tea

Dilute juice with tea and serve warm or cold.

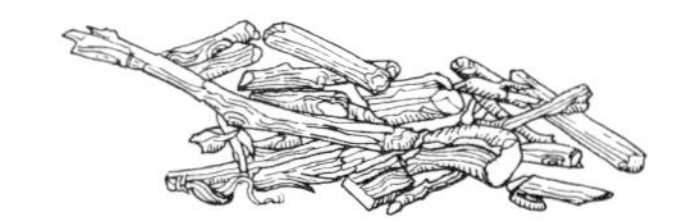

5 From 2 years onwards

The problem of differing tastes

By the time your child is 2 years old she has left babyhood behind. Her physical abilities are considerable: sitting and standing; running and climbing and avoiding obstacles; walking up and down stairs; playing happily alone for short periods of time with simple and more complex toys; recognizing objects and individuals from photographs or drawings in picture books. She no longer has to cry in order to communicate, her wishes can be put into words and you will be left in no doubt about what she does or does not like with regard to people, places or food. In some ways, this makes life easier. Your child now has a distinctive personality which not only reflects family traits but also reveals specific individual characteristics and preferences. This is particularly evident when it comes to food choice.

The need for flexibility

One child may differ very much from another or from her parents in which foods she likes and dislikes and this can present difficulties, especially where there are several children in a family and the possibility of differences in taste occurring is greater. However, parents of large families rarely have the time or resources to cater for individual tastes but a little flexibility and imagination can often enable problems to be circumvented.

It has already been pointed out that children will often eat a particular food if puréed or cooked with other ingredients, even if they reject it in its natural state, so with only a little extra effort, it is usually possible to cook the same basic ingredients for all the family and then make some minor adaptations before serving to make it acceptable to a child who dislikes eating it the way everyone else is having it. However, for practical purposes, every effort should be made as early as possible to encourage a liking for a wide range of foods. If certain foods cannot be taken by one member of the family because of a health problem either a more suitable substitute can be found and used by the whole family or the offending food can be omitted from main meals and served separately as an optional extra for other family members. If an important nutrient source is rejected by a child it is important to find an alternative (see Nutrient chart page 16).

Parties are special occasions but children enjoy funny face sandwiches and savouries as much as sweet treats

The junk food issue

The inclusion of highly flavoured, sweet and savoury processed foods and drinks in a child's diet usually blunts the appetite and upsets food choice at mealtimes. Most convenience foods are made to high standards of hygiene but few are meant, so the manufacturers say, to be eaten exclusively in place of fresh and wholefoods. Yet sadly for many adults and children these days, it is often fresh food that is the novelty. One of the best ways to ensure that your young family eats the best is to keep only 'healthy' food in the house – fruit, vegetables, nuts, seeds, raisins, home-made biscuits, breads and cakes, unsweetened fruit juices – that way the children can eat anything they like!

Supermarkets are improving

It is interesting to notice that over the last couple of years there has been an encouraging trend among major food manufacturers and retailers to produce and stock items which used to be considered of interest only to a minority market. Now, in many supermarkets, there are an increasing number of wholesome snacks and drinks available for children and adults – muesli bars with nuts, seeds and raisins, cereal and fruit bars, carob bars and carob-coated raisins and peanuts, pots of unsweetened plain or fruit yoghurt, low fat milks and cheeses. Some stock organically grown fruit and vegetables and increasingly you can select and weigh your own, and most have a very good supply of dry stores: fresh or toasted ground nuts or seeds, unsalted crisps and puffed rice cakes, rye crispbreads, whole wheat digestives, additive-free cereals, tinned fruit in unsweetened juice, unsalted tinned vegetables, cold-pressed oils, fish in olive oil or brine, tinned tomatoes and tomato purée.

At the same time it is worthwhile to establish a liking for home-made versions of some of the most popular convenience foods (e.g. baked beans, hamburgers, fish fingers, french fries, ice cream, fizzy drinks) so that you can be sure that no artificial colourings, flavourings and preservatives have been added. Hopefully when the packet or bottled versions are offered to your child they will taste quite different and not be as well liked as your own (see recipe section in this chapter for home-made versions of popular foods).

Invidious advertising

It must be said, however, that bringing up a child in an environment where processed foods and drinks are being constantly and persuasively advertised is no easy task. The advertisements placed between children's television programmes are almost exclusively aimed at the mini-market showing bright, happy, healthy children having fun whilst eating or drinking product A or B. The message is; 'If you want to have a good time and look like us, buy this product'. It works

Ice-cream does not have to be junk food; home-made from fresh ingredients, it can be a useful source of nutrients in the diet

with adults and is designed to work even more effectively on the impressionable minds of children. Much time may be required to persuade your child that they would be better off without the brightly coloured edibles being advertised, but all the arguments about harming the teeth and putting on weight just don't ring true compared with the image of delight and satisfaction conveyed by the advertisements.

Socializing

The older a child becomes the more difficult it is to have control over her eating habits. Friends in school may make fun of her for eating unsliced, wholemeal bread and home-made food; well-meaning relatives offer sweet and savoury treats and although many parents are aware of the importance of good nutrition they are unsure about what they should or could do to bring about necessary changes in current eating trends.

However strong your views about the need to avoid junk foods your child should not be made to feel fear or guilt about wanting or eating these products. Having been brought up on healthy food the occasional deviation will do no serious harm and it may be very important for your child to feel one of the crowd with her school friends. If this means eating school lunches and having the occasional packet of crisps or carton of squash then it is better than making her feel an outsider.

Children learn from experience

It is much better that the older child learns from personal experience that some foods are better for her than others. Suffering from a sore stomach, nausea, diarrhoea or toothache as a result of eating the wrong things is an effective way of learning that something is wrong. Offer appropriate sympathy and remind her that if she eats the right things it will be unlikely to happen again.

A child's own tastes must be allowed to develop. It is far better if she chooses to refuse an offered sweet than for a parent to answer in her place and say: 'She doesn't eat sweets.' If asked in advance what your child might like as a treat you can certainly offer suggestions (for instance, muesli, fruit or carob bars are a healthy alternative to conventional sweets) but choose foods that you know can be easily bought.

Shopping trips

When small, local food shops provided personal service and home deliveries, the problem of how to cope with the practicalities of buying and transporting food with young children in tow did not exist but now that the majority of privately run shops have closed and been replaced by large supermarkets, the daily trip to the shops has, in many cases, been replaced by a once-a-week visit to the supermarket and this, for all its apparent advantages, creates its own problems.

Tips to keep children occupied

Not the least of these problems is how to occupy young children while choosing goods. Wire trolleys fitted with baby/infant seats mean that your child is at just the right level to see what you are doing and to view the passing array of goodies. As your hand stretches out to pick something off a shelf so does hers – it is all a great game and it is very difficult to explain that it is a game only you can play. With a very young child a favourite toy is usually enough to take her attention away from what you are doing but with an older child, who recognizes that you are buying food, it is often a good idea to give her a small box of raisins or a tub of finger foods to keep mouth, stomach and hands busy while you whizz around the aisles, avoiding the areas where sweets and cakes are displayed.

Feeding hints when travelling

Travelling with children can present difficulties but short trips are seldom a problem whether by car or public transport. Fresh fruit, sandwiches, tubs of freshly cooked food packed in a wide-necked thermos flask or insulated cool box will satisfy most food needs. It is important to carry fresh water or a warm or cool drink with you as dehydration is often a cause of travel sickness.

If prone to travel sickness it is best not to give a child a large meal before setting off as the motion of the vehicle can cause rapid regurgitation. Fresh or stewed apples, soups, crisp and crunchy foods are the best things to eat before a journey. Safely strapped in to a car seat with a good view and plenty of ventilation a child is likely to be less prone to queasiness.

If you are travelling with a young baby you will want to check the availability of washing, changing and feeding facilities en route. Breastfeeding in public is not always culturally accepted but feeding rooms are often available in large train stations, motorway service stations, airports or on aeroplanes. It is a good idea to have a bag equipped with all the food, drinks, washing and changing equipment that may be needed by your baby which you can always take with you. This is particularly important when flying in case part of your luggage is temporarily misplaced or lost. Jars of baby food are very useful when travelling as the meal can be eaten straight from the jar and the leftovers thrown away and powdered baby foods can be easily made up using boiled water – make sure you take along appropriate utensils, dishes, cups or bottles. Bottle feeds will need to be made as required unless they can be prepared in advance and packed in an insulated bag with an ice pack but then a means of heating the feed will be needed so it is necessary to check in advance that this is available.

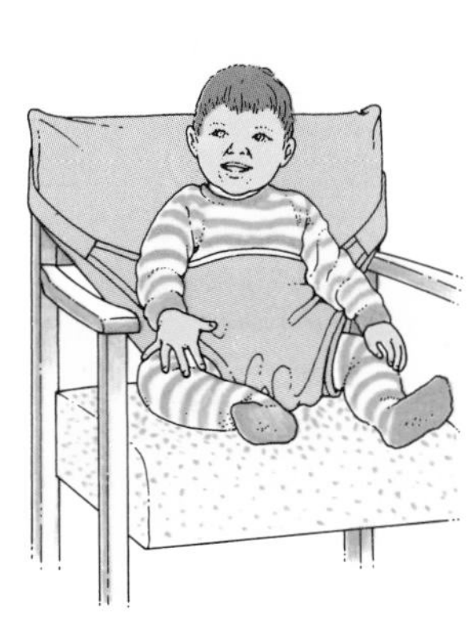

A fabric chair harness transforms most normal chairs when travelling or visiting

Long journeys

Most airlines allow parents with young children on to the aeroplane and into their seats before the other passengers and go out of their way to provide everything you need. Many have a stock of tinned or bottled baby foods and nappies etc. are available for emergencies. Crayons, colouring books and small toys are often given to young children by the airline to keep them occupied during the flight and they can take them with them when they leave if they want to. Bulkhead seats give more leg room and a play space for toddlers. Take a small blanket to cover the floor and make sure you have a selection of favourite toys. Most aeroplane food leaves a lot to be desired and is generally best avoided for younger children. Food poisoning is not unknown especially when the food on offer is shellfish or chicken. The combination of excitement, fizzy drinks, ice-cream

Long journeys can be very boring for older children so a good view, a favourite toy and a refreshing nibble to prevent dehydration are welcome distractions

and other inappropriate foods and drinks when travelling can often result in a stomach upset which could spoil part or all of the holiday. Children (and some adults) become grumpy if they miss their usual mealtimes so always carry food rations even if you do not expect to need them. There are frequently unexpected delays and seldom suitable catering facilities.

Before going abroad check with your doctor about the need for immunization and consult your travel agent about medical facilities in the country to which you are going. Try if possible to avoid travelling during peak holiday times as these often cause delays.

All children travel best when asleep and this is fairly easy to arrange with a very young baby, but be prepared to have to keep an older child occupied once the initial novelty of being on the move wears off. Try to avoid your child becoming over-excited as this can often end in tantrums and tears – the more organized the parents are, the calmer any journey will be.

Don't forget to take a moist cloth in a polythene/water-proof bag to wipe sticky fingers and spills and a first-aid kit (see page 109) is worth taking on even the shortest journey.

Always take one or two items that your child can recognize from home such as feeding dishes and utensils and don't forget to bring her favourite toy or 'cuddly', particularly if it helps her to go to sleep easily.

Party ideas

Birthday and festive occasions are fun to celebrate and although children are attracted by brightly-coloured, sweets, biscuits and cakes, savoury foods and sandwiches are also party favourites – in fact anything that can be eaten using fingers rather than utensils are usually very popular. Here are some suggestions to help make your party a success.

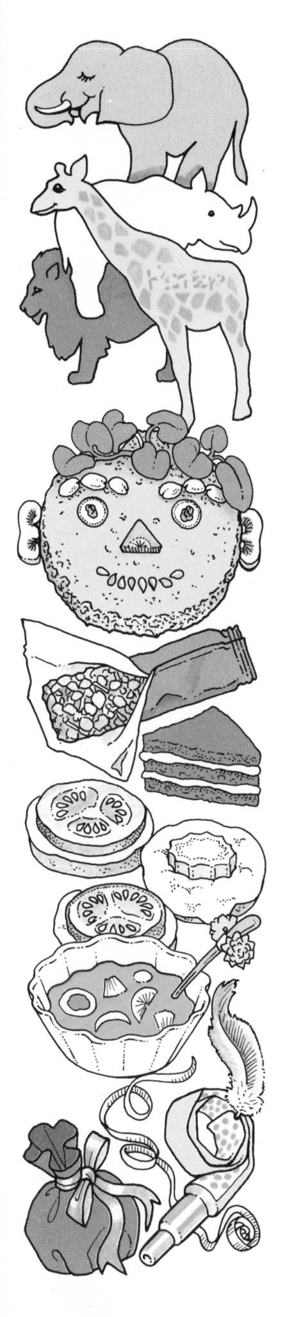

□ Choosing a party theme is a good idea. A favourite book, television series or hobby are all possibilities and an animal theme is always popular. Mark place settings with cards in the shape of zebras, elephants and tigers with the children's names written on one side.

□ A jungle trail mapped out on a paper table cloth can lead from a raw vegetable plate to the savouries, the fruit plates and lastly 'the cake'.

□ Open-face sandwiches can be great fun when you make circles of bread into people with vegetables and raisins for noses, eyes, ears and hair.

□ Other suitable savouries include triple-layer sandwiches with creamy, crunchy or salad fillings.

□ Soft-cooked millet grain rolled in toasted sesame seed meal, served hot or cold, make a change from fatty sausage rolls.

□ Tiny wholemeal scones toasted with finely grated, mild white cheese and slivers of tomato are easy to prepare and look like miniature pizzas.

□ In place of crisps, sweets and bought biscuits try pre-packed oat, honey, fruit and nut bars (available in supermarkets and wholefood shops), peanut or muesli biscuits, sesame dream sweets or carob chews and banana parcels.

□ Delicious rainbow jellies can be made from a variety of unsweetneed fruit juices and agar agar.

□ Fruit kebabs with home-made ice-cream are a novelty.

□ Lakes of unsweetened fruit juice diluted with naturally sparkling spring water can be made to look exciting with thin slices of fresh fruit floating on the surface. Serve this drink with a ladle decorated with paper flowers.

□ The birthday or festive cake need not be a heavy, sticky affair. In fact it need not be a cake at all as long as the decorations are not forgotten. A fancy frill can be fixed around a straight-sided circular bowl containing a home-made trifle topped with a thin layer of cream and appropriate candles or try a carrot cake topped with cream cheese and fruit.

□ Paper hats and table decorations are as much a part of the party excitement as the food. Little, brightly-coloured 'mystery bags' containing balloons, two or three home-made sweets and a miniature packet of raisins make cheap, easily prepared presents to give as going-home gifts.

The ubiquitous sandwich

The sandwich seems to appear on every occasion – from babies' birthday parties to businessmen's buffet lunches – as the ideal answer for a quick meal or party filler. They are undoubtedly here to stay so bearing in mind that commercial wheat may not be the best grain on which to base one's sandwiches, especially for young children, here are some alternative suggestions for breads and fillings to make a wonderful variety of open, closed, double or triple-decker sandwiches.

Breads

100% organic wholewheat bread □ Russian rye bread □ Pitta bread □ Sweet and sour rye bread □ Sourdough bread □ Pumpernickel □ Multi-grain and mixed grain breads □ Piima rice bread □ Essene bread made from sprouted grains □ Maize or corn bread □ Crispbreads □ Puffed brown rice 'cakes' □ Home-made mixed grain scones, crêpes, pancakes and pizza bases.

Sandwich fillings

□ Vegetable spreads – onion and carrot □ Pulse spreads – lentil, aduki bean, chickpea □ Nut and seed spreads – sesame, sunflower, almond and hazelnut □ Fruit spreads – no-sugar jam, apple sauce, avocado □ Tofu spreads □ Yeast extract used to flavour cooked beans or vegetable purée □ Boiled egg slices or omelette strips □ Grated white goat's, cow's or sheep's milk cheeses □ Minced roast chicken, beef or lamb □ Flaked cooked fish – sardines, salmon, mackerel, haddock □ Seasonal salad ingredients – ripe mini tomatoes, radishes, celery, cucumber, watercress, mustard cress, sprouted alfalfa, mung or aduki beans or whole lentils, raw mushrooms, sliced black olives, blanched red pepper, blanched fennel slivers, finely shredded Chinese leaves or home-grown lettuce and lacto-fermented pickles (not vinegar pickles).

Party sandwiches

Use mixed wholegrain bread or wholewheat bread. Cut the loaf into slices about 1.25 cm (½ in) thick, then spread with a wholesome filling from the following selection □ Peanut butter on its own or mixed with banana or grated apple □ Sunflower seed spread and cucumber slices □ Egg mayonnaise mixed with parsley and yoghurt □ Bean spread on its own or with cucumber slices □ Lentil spread on its own or mixed with mayonnaise □ Cottage cheese mixed with finely chopped dates or raisins □ Cheese spread.

Cut the filled sandwiches in circles, stars or other decorative shapes: leave some sandwiches open and decorate them with pieces of brightly coloured vegetable like carrot. For variety also use small wholemeal rolls cut in half, spread with a filling and left open.

Another different presentation is sliced bread spirals. Cut the loaf lengthwise and spread with filling, then roll up along its length. Wrap tightly in moist greaseproof paper and refrigerate for about 1 hour. Remove wrapping and cut the 'Swiss roll' into thin slices.

Snack suggestions

□ Fresh fruit salad or soaked sultanas with toasted flaked nuts or seeds □ Fresh dates □ Portions of seasonal fresh fruit □ Home-made, natural yoghurt with fresh or soaked dried fruit or toasted nuts □ Seasonal grated salad – coleslaw, carrot and beetroot or celery, apple and walnut □ Wholegrain or mixed grain bread or scone with nut or seed spread, lentil or bean spread and bean sprouts or seasonal salad filling □ Finger salad – carrot and celery sticks, cauliflower sprigs, the centre of broccoli stalks, crispy Kos lettuce home-grown, cucumber cubes □ Millet squares and salad □ Savoury brown rice salad □ Savoury brown rice with cooked vegetables □ Brown rice and toasted nuts or seeds □ Home-made crackers and biscuits with nut, savoury or fruit spreads □ Melon balls using watermelon, honey-dew melon or cantaloupe melon □ Seedless or peeled and seeded grapes □ Stoned cherries □ Whole strawberries Fresh pineapple rings □ Unsweetened fresh fruit juice diluted with an equal amount of water □ Nut milk or goat's milk carob drink.

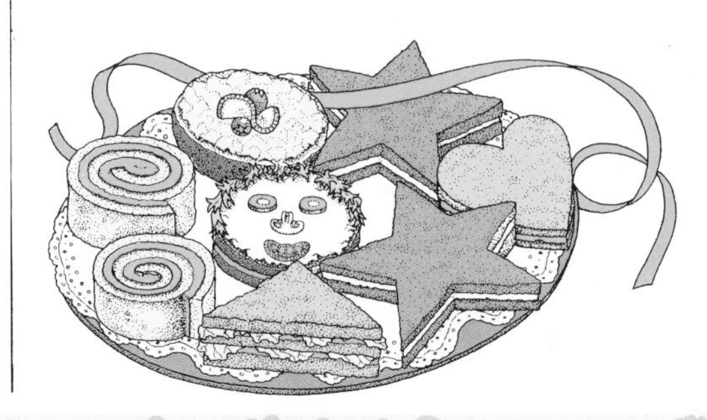

SESAME RYE CEREAL

(From 9 months. Serves 1)

1 rye crispbread
1 tsp light sesame tahini, unsalted

Spread crispbread with tahini, break into a bowl and stir in a little hot water to mix. Mash to a soft texture.

The flavour can be varied using sunflower seed spread, pure fruit purée or no-sugar jam, but do not use peanut butter as this is too oily and difficult to digest.

For a gluten-free cereal substitute a salt-free, puffed brown rice biscuit for the crispbread.

This is very easy to prepare and makes an ideal meal when travelling.

FLAKED MILLET SAVOURY

(From 9 months. Serves 1)

2 tbs millet flakes
2 tsps cooked lentils or beans (in emergency use tinned beans, thoroughly rinsed)
8 tbs boiling water

Place millet flakes and beans in flask and add boiling water. Stir once, to mix, using a wooden spoon. Put lid on flask and leave at least 15 minutes or up to 2 hours. Allow to cool before serving.

Another easy meal to prepare when away from home.

GLUTEN-FREE, SALT-FREE AND SUGAR-FREE CEREAL

(Serves 1)

Some manufacturers are producing puffed wholegrain cereals which are additive, sugar and salt-free. The grains used include brown rice, millet and maize (corn) all of which are gluten-free. Where these are not available, use 1–3 puffed brown rice 'cakes', salt-free variety. Crumble into a bowl and moisten with unsweetened fruit juice or milk plus sliced fresh fruit, stewed fruit or soaked dried fruit.

Serve as a breakfast cereal or as an instant meal when travelling and you can add toasted sunflower, sesame or almond meal for extra nourishment.

PULSE SPREADS

When used as the main protein source use pulses in the following proportions:

1 tbs cooked pulses (50–75 g/2–3 oz)
4 tbs cooked wholegrain (100 g/4 oz)

Good combinations □ Aduki beans and brown rice □ Chickpeas and millet □ Brown lentils and buckwheat noodles.

Cooked pulses can also be added to soups, meat casseroles and bean loaves. For sauces, purée and thicken with arrowroot or kuzu. Sieved, mashed or liquidized, with lightly steamed carrot, cauliflower, onion or leek, pulse spreads of different flavours and textures can be made to suit all ages. The addition of light sesame tahini adds extra nourishment.

LENTIL SPREAD

(Serves 4)

100 g (4 oz) cooked lentils, drained of stock
25 g (1 oz) light tahini
100 g (4 oz) cooked onion or leek, finely sliced
100 g (4 oz) cooked vegetable of choice (cauliflower, carrot, Brussels sprouts)
25 g (1 oz) finely chopped parsley

Sieve, mash or liquidize all ingredients. If made with all fresh ingredients this will keep in the refrigerator for 2–3 days. Serve hot or cold with wholegrain cereal such as millet or brown rice, or spread on fingers of toast or roll into balls and coat in almond meal.

Use whole brown lentils for a rich flavour. Finely grated carrot or carrot juice can be added during or after sieving.

Variations □ Aduki beans, cauliflower, carrot □ Chickpeas, leek, onion □ Black-eye beans, pumpkin, onion.

CARROT SPREAD

(Serves 6–8)

450 g (1 lb) carrots, diced
75 ml (3 fl oz) water
1–2 tsp oil
25 g (1 oz) fresh parsley, finely chopped

Warm pot and brush with oil. Toss carrots in pot to coat with oil then add water and simmer until tender. Mash or sieve and stir in parsley.

ONION SPREAD

(Serves 6–8)

450 g (1 lb) onions, very finely sliced
1–2 tsp sunflower or sesame oil
pinch sea salt or seaweed powder
50 ml (2 fl oz) water

Brush pot with oil and gently shallow fry onions sprinkled with seasoning (omit salt for babies under 12 months). Stir occasionally to prevent burning. After 15 minutes add water, cover and cook gently for 1 hour until mixture is very soft. Remove lid and simmer, stirring to remove any remaining liquid. Turn into a dish to cool and use in place of butter.

NUT AND SEED SPREADS

(Serves 2–3)

25 g (1 oz) almond or hazelnut butter or sunflower seed spread
75–100 g (3–4 oz) cooked vegetable
25 ml (1 fl oz) vegetable stock, carrot juice, unsweetened apple juice or finely grated carrot

Blend all ingredients to a smooth paste.

CHEESE SPREAD

(Serves 2–3)

50 g (2 oz) Cheddar, Edam or Gouda
50 g (2 oz) cottage cheese
2 tsp mayonnaise

Grate the hard cheese and mix all ingredients to a spreading consistency.

AVOCADO SPREAD

(Serves 4)

1 ripe avocado pear
125 g (5 oz) tofu soya bean curd
2–4 tsp freshly pressed lemon juice
6–8 puffed rice cakes, crispbreads or fingers of toast
25 g (1 oz) cucumber slivers or grated carrot (to garnish)

Blend tofu with avocado and lemon juice. Spread on toast or crispbread and serve at once. This spread does not keep well.

MISO SOUP

(Serves 6–8)

100 g (4 oz) onion, finely sliced
150–225 g (6–8 oz) cauliflower sprigs
50 g (2 oz) carrot, diced
900 ml (32 fl oz) water or kombu stock
2 tsp miso or less

Simmer onion in 1 cup of stock until tender. Add remaining vegetables and stock and cook for 10–15 minutes until vegetables are tender. Dilute miso in a little hot soup then turn down heat to simmering and add miso to pot. Do not allow to boil after adding miso. Turn off heat and allow flavours to blend.

Soup can be made in larger quantities but is best flavoured with miso as required. Store in refrigerator for up to 3 days in a covered bowl.

Vary the vegetables according to season or try adding some sea vegetables such as arame, dulse or wakame.

MEAL-IN-A-BOWL SOUP

(Serves 6–8)

To the basic miso soup add □ Cooked whole grain – brown rice, millet, soba or buckwheat noodles □ Cooked pulses □ Bean stock □ Cooked chicken or lamb.

Heat basic soup and additions thoroughly before adding miso.

POTATO STICKS

(Serves 4–6)

450 g (1 lb) large potatoes
570 ml (1 pint) cold pressed sunflower or corn oil
A little gomasio sesame salt or sesame seed meal or roasted seaweed powder

Scrub potatoes and leave unpeeled if home-grown. Slice into 0.6 cm (¼ in) thick diagonals, turn and slice into 0.6 cm (¼ in) thick matchsticks. Soak these in a large bowl of ice cold water for 2–3 hours. Drain and dry well. The 'sticks' can either be shallow or deep fried. Whichever method is used keep oil below smoking point. If shallow frying, brush pan with oil and toss sticks in batches over a medium heat. When cooked tip into heated dish lined with kitchen paper.

POTATO CRISPS

(Serves 6–8)

Use same ingredients as before. Scrub potatoes and leave unpeeled if home-grown. Slice very finely – a mandoline grater is best. Soak slivers in ice cold water for 3–4 hours. Drain thoroughly and pat dry. Deep fry in batches and drain on paper.

These can be stored in an airtight container. For older children sprinkle with diluted soya sauce and re-crisp in oven.

SARDINE OR SALMON PIZZA

(Serves 4)

Scone base

100 g (4 oz) barley and rye flour or organic wholewheat flour
1–1½ tsp home-made baking powder or ½ tsp each bicarbonate of soda and cream of tartar
25 g (1 oz) butter or oil
2–3 tbs water

Sift flour and raising agents, rub in butter or oil and add water to make a soft dough. Roll out to 1.25 cm (½ in) thickness and cut 4 rounds or shape to fit pie plate.

Filling

100 g (4 oz) onion, finely sliced
12 ml (½ fl oz) oil
50 g (2 oz) mushrooms, sliced
210 g (7½ oz) can sardines or
100 g (4 oz) can salmon
50 g (2 oz) grated white cheese
1 ripe tomato

Lightly fry onion and mushrooms for 2–3 minutes until softened. Spread mixture over pizza base, arrange sardines or flaked salmon on top and scatter with grated cheese. Slice tomato into rounds and place on top. Bake at 190°C (375°F)/Gas 5 for 20–25 minutes.

Alternative scone base – gluten-free

225 g (8 oz) mashed potato
1 beaten egg or 25 ml (1 fl oz) oil
brown rice flour to stiffen

Mix all ingredients well. Shape into 4 flat cakes 1.25 cm (½ in) thick or a single large round.

FISH FINGERS

(Serves 4)

225 g (8 oz) cooked fish, flaked
350 g (12 oz) boiled potato, mashed or 225 g (8 oz) potato + 100 g (4 oz) cooked brown rice (combine with mashed potato)
2 tbs freshly chopped parsley (optional)
1 ripe tomato, grilled or blanched and sieved (optional)
1–4 tsp tamari/shoyu soya sauce or pinch sea salt
1 egg, beaten
100 g (4 oz) fine rye breadcrumbs (use maize meal for gluten-free diet)

Combine fish, potato/rice, parsley and tomato. Gradually mix in egg, adding slightly more or less to make a moist but not over-soft mixture. Divide evenly into 10 pieces, form into 1.25 cm (½ in) thick rectangular 'fingers' and toss in breadcrumbs. Place on a baking tray in the oven at 180°C (350°F)/Gas 4 for 10 minutes or until golden. Alternatively, grill or shallow fry, turning to brown both sides.

The tomato can be omitted altogether or sliced and served raw as a simple salad with mustard cress or alfalfa sprouts.

KEDGEREE

(Serves 4–6)

225 g (8 oz) cold, steamed fish or
100 g (4 oz) cooked prawns
350 g (12 oz) cooked brown rice
1 hard boiled egg (optional)
100 g (4 oz) sweetcorn kernels
25 ml (1 fl oz) oil or 50 ml (2 fl oz) vegetable stock
pinch sea salt
1–2 tsp freshly chopped parsley

Flake fish taking great care to remove all bones. Chop egg into fine dice. Heat oil or stock in pan and add sweetcorn, additional vegetables may be added if wished (leek, bean sprouts, garden peas). Cook for 5–10 minutes until tender. Add rice, fish, egg and seasoning, stirring carefully until heated through. Serve sprinkled with parsley. For a richer flavoured and heavier dish suitable for an older child – stir in 75 g (3 oz) yoghurt to mixture when heated, place in heatproof dish, scatter with finely grated white cheese, garnish with thin slices of tomato and brown under grill.

POT NOODLES WITH SUNFLOWER SEED SAVOURIES

(Serves 4–6)

225 g (8 oz) packet buckwheat or soba noodles + a 15 cm (6 in) kombu seaweed (optional)
25 ml (1 fl oz) sesame or olive oil
50 g (2 oz) spring onions/scallions, sliced
50 g (2 oz) mung bean or aduki bean sprouts
50 g (2 oz) vegetable of choice (broccoli sprigs, cauliflower sprigs, garden peas, sweetcorn kernels, French/green beans)
50 g (2 oz) Chinese leaves or crisp home-grown lettuce, finely shredded
100 g (4 oz) dehusked sunflower seeds
4 tsp tamari/shoyu soya sauce diluted with 2 tsp water

Following instructions on noodle packet, bring pot of water to boil and add strip of kombu (this adds calcium and other minerals to the noodles and improves their flavour). Add noodles either whole or broken into even lengths (makes eating easier but not so much fun), turn down heat and simmer for 10 minutes until cooked. To test remove a noodle and break off one end – the colour should be the same all the way through. Drain through sieve, keeping cooking water for sauces, soups or baking. Use immediately or rinse with cold water to prevent further cooking. Meanwhile heat oil in shallow pot and lightly cook vegetables starting with onions, then the hardest vegetable, then the peas and bean sprouts. Keep as crunchy as possible but if not accepted this way by younger family members leave some of the mixture a little longer to soften. Turn into a pre-heated dish lined with kitchen paper and keep warm.

Toast or dry roast sunflower seeds until golden. Remove from heat and stir in soya sauce and water. Return to heat if necessary whilst coating seeds to help them dry. Set aside to cool.

Pre-heat oven to 180°C (350°F)/Gas 4. Layer noodles and cooked vegetables in lightly oiled baking dish. Cover and heat through for 15–20 minutes. Serve in little bowls (or paper cups) scattered with sunflower seeds and a saucerful of shredded Chinese leaves.

HIGHLAND FRIED CHICKEN

(Serves 4)

Chicken portions (1–2 per person depending on size)
50 g (2 oz) fine oatmeal
1 tsp dried sage
pinch sea salt or dried seaweed powder
125 ml (5 fl oz) milk or 1 beaten egg

Mix oatmeal, herb and seasoning. Dip chicken in milk or egg and coat in oatmeal mixture. Shallow fry tossing in oil to brown then place in an ovenproof baking dish in a pre-heated oven at 180°C (350°F)/Gas 4 for 30 minutes or longer depending on size of portions.

Serve with pre-boiled, sliced and shallow fried potatoes or brown rice and a leafy salad or lightly steamed broccoli or Brussels sprouts.

BEEF AND BEAN SLICE OR MEAT LOAF

(Serves 4–6)

100 g (4 oz) minced beef or lamb
50 g (2 oz) lamb's liver, minced
50 g (2 oz) cooked beans of choice
100 g (4 oz) onion, diced
1 stalk celery, diced and/or 50 g (2 oz) grated carrot
100 g (4 oz) cooked brown rice or rye or organic wholewheat breadcrumbs or oatflakes
25 ml (1 fl oz) oil
1 egg
pinch sea salt
1 ripe tomato, sieved or 1 tsp tomato purée (optional)
pinch mixed dried herbs (optional)

Leave beans whole or mash. Lightly shallow fry vegetables with salt and herbs and add to beans with rice or breadcrumbs. Toss meats in same pot to brown then add to mixture with tomato and egg. The mixture should be moist (add a little bean stock if over-dry). Put in loaf tin brushed with oil and bake at 180°C (350°F)/Gas 4 for 40 minutes.

This makes a very warming winter dish served hot with arrowroot gravy and lightly steamed green vegetables or in summer, it can be served cold, in slices, with salad. Alternatively, the mixture can be steamed rather than baked – place in a covered steaming bowl and cook for 1 hour.

BEEFBURGERS

(Serves 4)

225 g (8 oz) minced beef
100 g (4 oz) onion, finely diced
pinch sea salt
25 g (1 oz) flour (barley, organic wholewheat, brown rice, soya, fine oatmeal)
½ egg (optional)
25 ml (1 fl oz) oil

Beat egg. Combine with all other ingredients except oil. Divide into 4 burgers. Shallow fry or grill, brushed lightly with oil. Serve with boiled potatoes or brown rice or for a picnic in a rye or organic wholewheat bread roll with crunchy, coleslaw salad.

BASMATTI RICE

(Serves 4)

Best quality white rice grown in the foothills of the Himalayas, basmatti has a delicate flavour which is enhanced by the addition of a little olive or sesame oil, in cooking.

150 g (6 oz) basmatti rice
350 ml (12 fl oz) water
25 ml (1 fl oz) oil
pinch sea salt (optional)

Rinse rice 2–3 times. Drain and add measured water, oil and salt. Cover, bring to boil then simmer for 20 minutes until all water is absorbed. Spoon gently into warmed serving dish separating grains as you do so.

NB Do not stir during cooking.

BASMATTI LENTILS

(Serves 4)

150 g (6 oz) cooked green lentils
225 g (8 oz) spinach or spring cabbage
225 g (8 oz) cooked basmatti rice

Rinse spinach and cook quickly in covered pot for 3–5 minutes. Drain and reserve liquid. Purée spinach and cooking water with lentils. Serve hot or cold in little bowls on a bed of rice. If using cabbage, finely shred and steam cook then purée with lentils. The contrasting green and white is highlighted when served with carrots or carrot and beetroot salad.

BOSTON STYLE BEANS

(Serves 4)

150 g (6 oz) black-eye beans, pre-soaked
150 g (6 oz) carrot, diced
150 g (6 oz) cauliflower sprigs
100 g (4 oz) broccoli sprigs, cabbage greens or Brussel sprouts, sliced
100 g (4 oz) onion or leek
12 ml (½ fl oz) blackstrap molasses
50 g (2 oz) celery, sliced
pinch dried herbs

Cook beans by standard recipe (see page 122), adding vegetables, herbs and molasses after 30 minutes. Cook a further 15–20 minutes, then drain off stock and thicken with arrowroot or kuzu. Pour over bean mixture and serve with grain of choice. It is very good with buckwheat noodles.

BOSTON BEAN SPREAD

(Serves 4–6)

Follow the recipe for Boston style beans halving the quantity of vegetables used. When cooked, drain off stock and continue cooking over a gentle heat to thicken. Stir to prevent burning. Transfer to a bowl to cool and use as a spread on crispbread or toast or roll in toasted seed meal and serve with salad.

SAVOURY TOFU CRÊPE FILLING OR GRAIN TOPPING

(Serves 4–6)

1–2 tsp oil
50 g (2 oz) each, onion, celery, tomato pulp, cauliflower (in tiny sprigs), finely sliced
pinch basil herb
1 tsp miso, dissolved in a little water
100 g (4 oz) tofu, diced
25 g (1 oz) feta cheese (optional)

Warm pot and brush with oil. Add onion and cook until tender. Add celery and cauliflower and cook for 3 minutes. Add tofu, mix well, cook for 3 minutes then add tomato, basil and miso. Cover and simmer for 5 minutes. Thicken if required with a little arrowroot or kuzu or simply stir in cheese and serve in freshly made crêpes.

ADUKI BOLOGNESE

(Serves 4–6)

Alternatively, serve savoury tofu sauce with freshly cooked grain such as millet or brown rice or stir in 100 g (4 oz) cooked aduki beans and serve with buckwheat noodles.

APPLE BEAN BAKE

(Serves 4–6)

Use aduki beans in the Boston style bean recipe. Purée to make a sauce and pour over sliced, well-flavoured eating apples in an ovenproof casserole. Bake for 20–30 minutes at 180°C (350°F)/Gas 4. This makes a remarkably good combination of flavours.

THE DREADED NUT CUTLET

(Makes 12 approx.)

100 g (4 oz) peanuts, almonds or sunflower seeds
100 g (4 oz) hazelnuts
100 g (4 oz) cashew nuts
225 g (8 oz) onion, finely sliced
25 ml (1 fl oz) oil
2 hard boiled, standard eggs
50 g (2 oz) each boiled carrot and potato
rye breadcrumbs or light sesame seeds to coat

Toast nuts lightly and remove skins. Add 1 tsp of diluted shoyu or tamari sauce for older tastes. Mince or blend nuts until fine. Shallow fry onion in oil, then blend all ingredients until smooth. Mould into rounds or cutlets and toss in coating. Bake as required at 180°C (350°F)/Gas 4 for 15 minutes. The mixture keeps well in the refrigerator for 1–3 days.

Serve hot or cold with salad or to extend a chicken dish in place of stuffing. A sure success despite their reputation.

CARROT MILK DRESSING

(Serves 4)

75 g (3 oz) finely grated carrot
75 ml (3 fl oz) soya milk
25 g (1 oz) sesame seeds

Blend and use as salad dressing or stir in cooked grain.

GLUTEN-FREE SAVOURY SAUCE

(Serves 4)

50 g (2 oz) arrowroot or kuzu
570 ml (1 pint) water, vegetable, bean or kombu stock
pinch dried or 2 tsp freshly chopped herb of choice (optional)
tamari, shoyu, miso or yeast extract to taste (omit for babies under 12 months)

Heat and adjust the flavour of the stock. Dissolve arrowroot or kuzu in a little cold liquid. Add to pot and stir over heat to thicken. The mixture will turn from cloudy to clear. Stir in herbs.

1 tsp freshly grated ginger juice can be added with the flavouring. Ginger aids the digestion of oily food and brassica vegetables (cabbage and sprouts). Pre-cooked vegetables can be added to sauce – fennel, for instance, is particularly good with fish.

ORGANIC WHOLEGRAIN SAUCE

(Serves 4)

25 g (1 oz) organic wholewheat, barley or rye flour
25 ml (1 fl oz) unrefined oil
570 ml (1 pint) stock as above
25 g (1 oz) finely chopped fresh parsley or simmered mushrooms (diced) or finely grated feta cheese

Heat oil and stir in flour to form a pastry ball. Remove from heat and gradually add stock. Return to heat, stirring until thickened. Add parsley or other flavouring and serve.

TOFU DRESSING

(Serves 20)

150 g (6 oz) grated carrot
50 g (2 oz) fresh parsley
225 g (8 oz) tofu
100 ml (4 fl oz) olive, sesame, sunflower oil or tahini
50 ml (2 fl oz) tamari sauce
pinch dill seed

Blend all ingredients until smooth. Use this dressing sparingly over very finely shredded raw vegetables or lightly steamed vegetables.

EGGLESS MAYONNAISE

(Serves 20)

175 ml (6 fl oz) olive oil
175 ml (6 fl oz) water
75 g (3 oz) soya milk powder
pinch sea salt (optional)
1 tbs lemon juice
50 ml (2 fl oz) apple cider vinegar
pinch dill seed (optional)

Blend soya powder and water. Gradually add oil one drop at a time, as for mayonnaise, with the blender on high speed. Reduce speed and add remaining ingredients. Pour into sterilized jar or bottle and store in refrigerator. Use within 10 days.

TOMATO SAUCE

(Serves 4–6)

350 g (12 oz) ripe tomatoes, home-grown
50 ml (2 fl oz) olive or sesame oil
50 g (2 oz) finely sliced salad onion
1 tbs lemon juice
25 ml (1 fl oz) tamari sauce
1 tsp kelp powder
pinch mixed dried herbs
25 g (1 oz) arrowroot or kuzu
25 ml (1 fl oz) water

Gently shallow fry onion in oil with kelp and herbs until soft. Stir in tomatoes and cook for 10 minutes. Sieve or strain to remove tomato skin and pips. Add lemon juice and tamari. Dissolve arrowroot in water. Put all ingredients in pot and stir over heat to thicken. Pour into serving jug or sterilized jars. Cool, cover and keep in refrigerator for up to 7 days.

This sauce can be poured over wholegrain rice, pasta, buckwheat noodles or steamed vegetables.

ROOT JUICE AND CUCUMBER DRESSING

(Serves 10)

50 g (2 oz) cucumber
50 g (2 oz) grated carrot
50 g (2 oz) grated beetroot
100 ml (4 fl oz) water

Blend and use over finely shredded raw or steamed vegetables.

NO-SUGAR JAMS

(Serves 6–8)

225 g (8 oz) fresh seasonal fruit (blackcurrant, apricot, peach)
50 ml (2 fl oz) unsweetened apple juice concentrate
50 g (2 oz) arrowroot or kuzu dissolved in 25 ml (1 fl oz) water

Simmer fruit in juice concentrate until soft, add arrowroot and stir to thicken, then reduce liquid by cooking for a further 15–20 minutes. Pot into sterilized jars and store in refrigerator for up to 7 days.

HONEY CURD

(Makes one, 225 g (8 oz) jar)

100 ml (4 fl oz) honey
100 g (4 oz) butter
1 standard egg
juice of one lemon

Put all ingredients in a heatproof bowl, place in a pot quarter filled with water which has been brought to the boil. Keep water simmering and stir mixture to thicken (about 15 minutes). Be careful not to boil or mixture will curdle. Pour into a sterilized glass jar and leave to set, covered with waxed paper. Keep in refrigerator and use within 4–5 days.

BANANA SEED BLEND

(Serves 4)

75 g (3 oz) ripe banana
100 ml (4 fl oz) sultana or apricot soaking water
25 g (1 oz) sesame seeds

Blend and use as a topping or sauce.

APRICOT ALMOND CREAM

(Serves 3–4)

150 g (6 oz) pre-soaked apricots plus water
75 g (3 oz) blanched almonds, finely ground
1 tbs sunflower oil

Liquidize all ingredients to make a dessert.

FUDGE CAKES

(Makes 18)

150 g (6 oz) brown rice flour
100 g (4 oz) soya flour
75 g (3 oz) carob powder
150 g (6 oz) chopped nuts or sultanas
40 g (1½ oz) bean flour
1½ tsp baking powder
200 ml (7 fl oz) water
75 ml (3 fl oz) brown rice syrup
40 ml (1½ fl oz) oil
1 tsp real vanilla essence

Combine all dry ingredients. Blend syrup, oil, vanilla and water and gradually stir into dry ingredients mixing well. Pour into lightly oiled cake tin or half fill individual bun tins. Bake for 30–40 minutes (20–30 minutes for buns) at 170°C (325°F)/Gas 3.

A-MAIZE-ING CAKE

350 g (12 oz) soya flour
350 g (12 oz) maize meal
4 tsp baking powder
425 ml (15 fl oz) diluted apple juice
40 ml (1½ fl oz) oil
25 ml (1 fl oz) brown rice syrup

Blend oil, juice and syrup. Combine all dry ingredients and gradually add liquid. Mix well. Pour into two oiled, floured, 22 cm (9 in) cake tins. Bake for 20–25 minutes at 190°C (375°F)/Gas 5. Test with skewer and if tacky leave a further 3–5 minutes.

When cool sandwich with no-sugar jam or fruit purée – apple, apricot and blackcurrant are favourites.

FINE CRÊPES

(Makes 18)

100 g (4 oz) organic wholewheat flour
50 g (2 oz) buckwheat or barley flour
1 egg (optional)
350 ml (12 fl oz) water
25 ml (1 fl oz) oil
2 tsp baking powder (optional)

Blend all ingredients except oil to a thick batter. Lightly oil a heated omelette pan. Cover base thinly with batter and turn when bubbles burst.

PANCAKES

(Makes 16)

75 g (3 oz) maize meal
75 g (3 oz) soya flour
150 ml (6 fl oz) water
25 ml (1 fl oz) oil
25 ml (1 fl oz) brown rice syrup

Blend all ingredients. Drop in tablespoon amounts on to heated, oiled, shallow pan. Turn when bubbles burst and cook until golden.

A grated apple or 100 g (4 oz) apple purée or finely grated carrot can be added to basic recipe.

CAROB DROPS

(Makes 20)

75 g (3 oz) carob chips
25 ml (1 fl oz) brown rice syrup or barley malt
½ tsp real vanilla essence
15 g (½ oz) muscovado sugar
225 g (8 oz) walnuts, sunflower seeds, flaked almonds or hazelnuts or
100 g (4 oz) each nuts or seeds and raisins or 225 g (8 oz) pre-soaked dried raisins, apricots, pears or peaches.

Put carob chips, syrup and sugar in bowl inside pot half filled with water or use double boiler. Heat to melt carob. Remove from heat and stir in vanilla, fruit and nuts. Drop in teaspoon amounts on to rice paper. Chill in refrigerator to set then store in airtight container.

MINI-SPONGES

(Makes 10)

100 g (4 oz) butter
75 ml (3 fl oz) brown rice syrup
100 g (4 oz) flour, organic wholewheat self-raising or rye and barley + 1 tsp baking powder
2 standard eggs

Cream butter and syrup until fluffy. Whisk eggs with a fork then beat into butter mixture. Gradually add flour to make a soft sponge mixture. Turn into lightly oiled and floured bun tins and bake on the middle shelf at 190°C (375°F)/Gas 5 for 12 minutes.

Optional extras □ 25 g (1 oz) carob chips □ 25 g (1 oz) raisins □ 1 tsp finely grated lemon rind.

BASIC WHOLEMEAL PASTRY

(Serves 4–6)

225 g (8 oz) barley, rye or organic wholewheat flour
125 g (5 oz) oil or butter
50 ml (2 fl oz) ice cold water

Sieve flour to remove roughest bran flakes. Mix flour and oil to form a breadcrumb mix and work in water to make a smooth dough. Halve the mixture and roll out thinly. In warm weather let pastry sit in refrigerator for 30 minutes between mixing and rolling. Bake wholemeal pastry in a hot oven 200°C (400°F)/Gas 6 for 15–35 minutes depending on size of pie or pasty.

Pastry fillings □ Cut pastry into saucer-sized circles for sweet or savoury turnovers or pasties and cut into teacup-sized circles for mini pie crusts or fold over and fill with almond meal and apricot jam or lentil spread and steamed vegetables.
□ Substitute 25 g (1 oz) seed meal for 25 g (1 oz) flour. Roll out thinly, prick and cut into biscuit shapes.
□ Use pastry to wrap small eating apples cored and filled with nuts and dried fruit.
□ Roll into a rectangle. Spread surface with apple and sultana and toasted, flaked almond mix. Roll up sealing the edges with water and bake as for pie to make a strudel.
□ A savoury strudel or mini pies can be made using a bean and vegetable mixture, minced chicken or saucy fish flakes.

GLUTEN-FREE PIE CRUST

(Serves 4–6)

100 g (4 oz) soya and bean flours
50 g (2 oz) brown rice flour
50 g (2 oz) sunflower seed meal
75 ml (3 fl oz) oil
25 ml (1 fl oz) brown rice syrup (optional)
75–100 ml (3–4 fl oz) ice cold water
pinch sea salt (optional)

Combine all dry ingredients. Stir in oil, water and syrup to bind, press into pie mould (this is a difficult mixture to roll) or roll between greaseproof paper to 0.6 cm (¼ in) thickness. Cut into small rounds to line bun tins or make animal shapes and bake as biscuits for 15 minutes at 180°C (350°F)/Gas 4.

CRUMBLE TOPPINGS

(Serves 4)

Flour or flake crumble

100 g (4 oz) organic wholewheat, barley or rye flour or
75 g (3 oz) flour
25 g (1 oz) sunflower or sesame seed meal
100 ml (4 fl oz) oil
50 ml (2 fl oz) brown rice syrup (optional)

Rub oil into flour or flakes and stir in sweetener. The omission of syrup and addition of a pinch of herbs makes an excellent savoury topping for casseroles.

Alternative topping – gluten free

100 g (4 oz) mixed bean flours
100 g (4 oz) mixed brown rice and maize flours
50–75 ml (2–3 fl oz) oil
1 tsp baking powder (optional)

Combine all dry ingredients and rub in oil.

Bake crumbles for 20–30 minutes until golden at 180°C (350°F)/Gas 4 for flour crumbles and 170°C (325°F)/Gas 3 for gluten-free mixes.

FESTIVE PIES OR CRUMBLE

(Serves 4–6)

100 g (4 oz) short crust or gluten-free pastry (use half for base and half for top of pies) or
50 g (2 oz) crumble topping of choice

Filling

350 g (12 oz) cooking or eating apples
40 g (1½ oz) sultanas or apricots
1 tbs brown rice syrup
1 tbs lemon juice
40 ml (1½ fl oz) water
pinch cinnamon
15 g (½ oz) arrowroot (optional)

Stew apple slices and dried fruit in water, lemon juice and syrup until tender. Drain off juice. Sieve, mash or leave apples whole and stir in cinnamon.

Use this mixture as a filling for autumnal apple pies, crumbles or a delicate summer mousse, made by folding in a well-beaten egg white. Glaze open pies with the drained cooking liquid, thickened with arrowroot.

LEMON AND PEAR PIES

(Makes 10)

10 pre-baked mini pie crusts
300 g (10 oz) fresh pear, peeled and cored
75 ml (3 fl oz) apple juice
275 ml (½ pint) water including drained juice from poached pears
100 g (4 oz) arrowroot
50 g (2 oz) ground cashews or sesame seed meal
rind and juice of 1 lemon
25 ml (1 fl oz) brown rice syrup
25 g (1 oz) agar agar flakes

Poach pears in apple juice, drain and dice. Blend remaining ingredients firstly dissolving arrowroot and agar agar in a little water. Put in pot and stir over heat to thicken. Divide pear between pie crusts and cover with warm mixture. Leave to cool.

YOGHURT ICE-CREAM

(Serves 4–6)

275 ml (10 fl oz) home-made goat's milk or cow's milk yoghurt
300 g (10 oz) ripe, seasonal soft fruit or soaked dried fruit
25–50 ml (1–2 fl oz) concentrated unsweetened apple juice to sweeten, if required

Blend yoghurt with fruit and juice and turn into a shallow container. Place in deep-freeze. Remove and stir thoroughly every 30 minutes until set. Remove from freezer 30 minutes before serving to soften slightly. Do not re-freeze once melted. Top with toasted flaked hazelnuts or flakes of carob chocolate or serve with fresh fruit.

ICE STICKS

(Serves 4)

225 ml (8 fl oz) unsweetened fruit juice, diluted to taste or
100 ml (4 fl oz) each of natural yoghurt and fruit juice or fruit pulp

Blend liquids. Pour into small rectangular ice moulds, placing a flat wooden stick in each. Freeze until solid.

This is a colour-free, sugar-free treat.

POP CORN

(Serves 2–4)

50 g (2 oz) popping corn
1 tbs oil (corn, sunflower or sesame)

A heavy saucepan with a tight-fitting lid is essential for this recipe. Place oil in pan to heat (keep below smoking point). Add corn and cover immediately with lid. Keep the corn moving by shaking the pan over the heat and keep the heat low to prevent burning. DO NOT REMOVE LID UNTIL POPPING STOPS. Toss in warmed honey or barley malt or sprinkle with diluted tamari or shoyu soya sauce or leave plain and use as a breakfast cereal with soaked sultanas and toasted flaked nuts or seeds.

BANANA PARCELS

(Serves 4)

½–1 very small banana per serving
100 g (4 oz) pastry per 4 bananas
25 g (1 oz) dehusked sesame seeds

Roll out pastry to 0.6 cm (¼ in) thickness. Cut into rectangles and roll around freshly peeled bananas, enclosing ends. Roll one side in sesame seeds and place on baking tray. Bake at 220°C (425°F)/Gas 8 for 8–10 minutes until golden. Serve warm or cold.

This makes a very good travel food.

APRICOT SQUARES

(Makes 12)

50 ml (2 fl oz) water
12 g (½ oz) barley or organic wholewheat flour
1 tbs barley malt or brown rice syrup
75 g (3 oz) sultanas, pre-soaked and minced
75 g (3 oz) dried apricots, pre-soaked and minced
50 g (2 oz) skimmed milk powder or goat's milk powder or soya flour (pre-cooked)
50 g (2 oz) dehusked sesame seeds or mixed crushed nuts and seeds
40 g (1½ oz) organic wheatgerm (optional)

Boil the first three ingredients for 5 minutes then remove from heat and add remaining ingredients. Form into small squares and toss in sesame seeds or toasted coconut.

MUESLI SQUARES

(Makes 25)

100 g (4 oz) raisins, dried apricots, dates or prunes
125 ml (5 fl oz) hot water
100 g (4 oz) oat flakes
50 g (2 oz) barley flakes
25 g (1 oz) flaked hazelnuts, almonds or peanuts
25 g (1 oz) sunflower or sesame seeds
50 ml (2 fl oz) vegetable oil
pinch sea salt

Soak dried fruit in hot water for 20 minutes. Strain off water into oil. Mix dry ingredients and chop. Add soaked fruit, stir in water and oil to make a moist dough. Press into baking tray to thickness of about 0.6 cm (¼ in) and bake 30–40 minutes in pre-heated oven at 150°C (300°F)/Gas 2. Cut into squares in tin and allow to cool.

PARTY CARROT CAKE

175 g (7 oz) organic wholewheat flour
2 rounded tsp home-made baking powder
100 g (4 oz) finely grated carrot
100 g (4 oz) butter
100 g (4 oz) muscovado sugar
grated rind of lemon or orange (optional)
2 standard eggs, lightly beaten
25 ml (1 fl oz) milk

Sift flour and baking powder to mix. Add carrot. In a separate bowl cream butter and sugar until soft and fluffy. Add rind, then eggs, gradually, beating well. Gently incorporate flour mixture and if required use the milk to make a soft mixture. Lightly grease and flour a circular cake tin 16 cm (6 in) and fill two-thirds with cake mixture. Bake in a pre-heated oven 160°C (325°F)/Gas 3 for 45–60 minutes.

CHEESE AND FRUIT TOPPING FOR CAKE

150 g (6 oz) curd or cottage cheese
75 g (3 oz) fruit purée
75 g (3 oz) whole fruit to decorate

Sieve cheese and mix two-thirds of it with puréed fruit. Halve cake and spread with filling. Use remainder of cheese to cover top of cake and decorate with pieces of fresh fruit.

SUNFLOWER ROLLS

(Makes 12)

225 g (8 oz) sunflower seeds
25 g (1 oz) honey or soaked dried fruit
50 g (2 oz) peanut butter
⅛ tsp vanilla essence (optional)
50 g (2 oz) grated coconut (for coating)

Lightly toast the sunflower seeds and blend to a fine meal. Mix in honey or chopped dried fruit, peanut butter and vanilla. Work until smooth and form into rolls about 2.5 cm (1 in) in diameter. Toast coconut and toss rolls in coating.

NUT DELIGHT

(Makes 20)

100 g (4 oz) sesame seeds
75 g (3 oz) finely shredded coconut
25 g (1 oz) light tahini
1½ tbs brown rice syrup
40 g (1½ oz) flaked or chopped almonds
25 g (1 oz) apricots, pre-soaked
¼ tsp real vanilla essence

Pre-heat oven to 150°C (300°F)/Gas 2. Combine all ingredients and mix well. Vary the texture from very smooth to chewy. Press into lightly oiled shallow baking tin to 1.25 cm (½ in) thickness and bake for 20 minutes to set. Cool and cut into 5 cm (2 in) fingers.

FRUIT AND NUT TREATS

(Makes 24)

75 g (3 oz) dried apricots
75 g (3 oz) pitted dates
75 g (3 oz) sultanas or raisins
75 g (3 oz) chopped walnuts
75 g (3 oz) very finely shredded coconut, sesame or sunflower seeds
1 tsp lemon juice or apple juice

Soak dried fruits in just enough boiling water to cover for 20 minutes. Drain and blend or grind fruit and nuts, stir in juice, form mixture into whole, walnut-sized pieces, roll in coconut or crushed seeds. Place on baking tray and chill. Store in airtight container.

These and the recipes above all make excellent sweet treats for parties, picnics and other special occasions.

6 Dietary problems

Health problems and diet

If your child is diagnosed as having a health problem and prescribed a special diet, this can, at first, seem like an overwhelming disaster and cause great concern over the child's future health; but try to remain calm. Reliable professional help and guidance is available to explain and advise you on what dietary changes are needed. Back-up support will be provided so that any problems you have can be discussed as they crop up and in the following weeks and months your child's progress will be carefully monitored. If you think your child has a dietary problem consult your health visitor or doctor for advice.

In most cases a change in diet means a rapid improvement in health which is adequate compensation for any extra effort you have had to make and as time goes on you may find that much of the general advice given concerning the child's special diet also applies to the rest of the family. If this is the case most family meals can be planned to incorporate the special dietary stipulations. After all, avoiding sugar, eating fresh wholefoods, high in fibre, low in fat and low in salt, and avoiding processed foods with artificial colourings, flavourings and preservatives is the basis of all sound nutrition and the theme of this book.

Illness can often be cured by diet

Much of the ill health experienced by adults and children is preventable and curable by a change in diet. Some diet-related, health problems are tooth decay, gum disease, obesity, constipation, diarrhoea, stomach upsets, ulcers, indigestion, skin problems, eczema, proneness to infection, coughs, colds, sinusitis, migraine and behavioural problems.

Conditions such as diabetes mellitus and Coeliac disease have genetic origins and their management requires specialist advice and care. If a child requires a special diet the cooperation of both parents is essential to help the child feel as normal as possible. This is particularly important when the child is mixing socially with other children and when foods offered are not always suitable. A child should never be made to feel an invalid because of his special dietary needs and, in most cases, general health, stamina and fitness will be better as a result of his avoidance of refined and processed foods.

Extra care and patience is needed when a child is sick or has a dietary problem

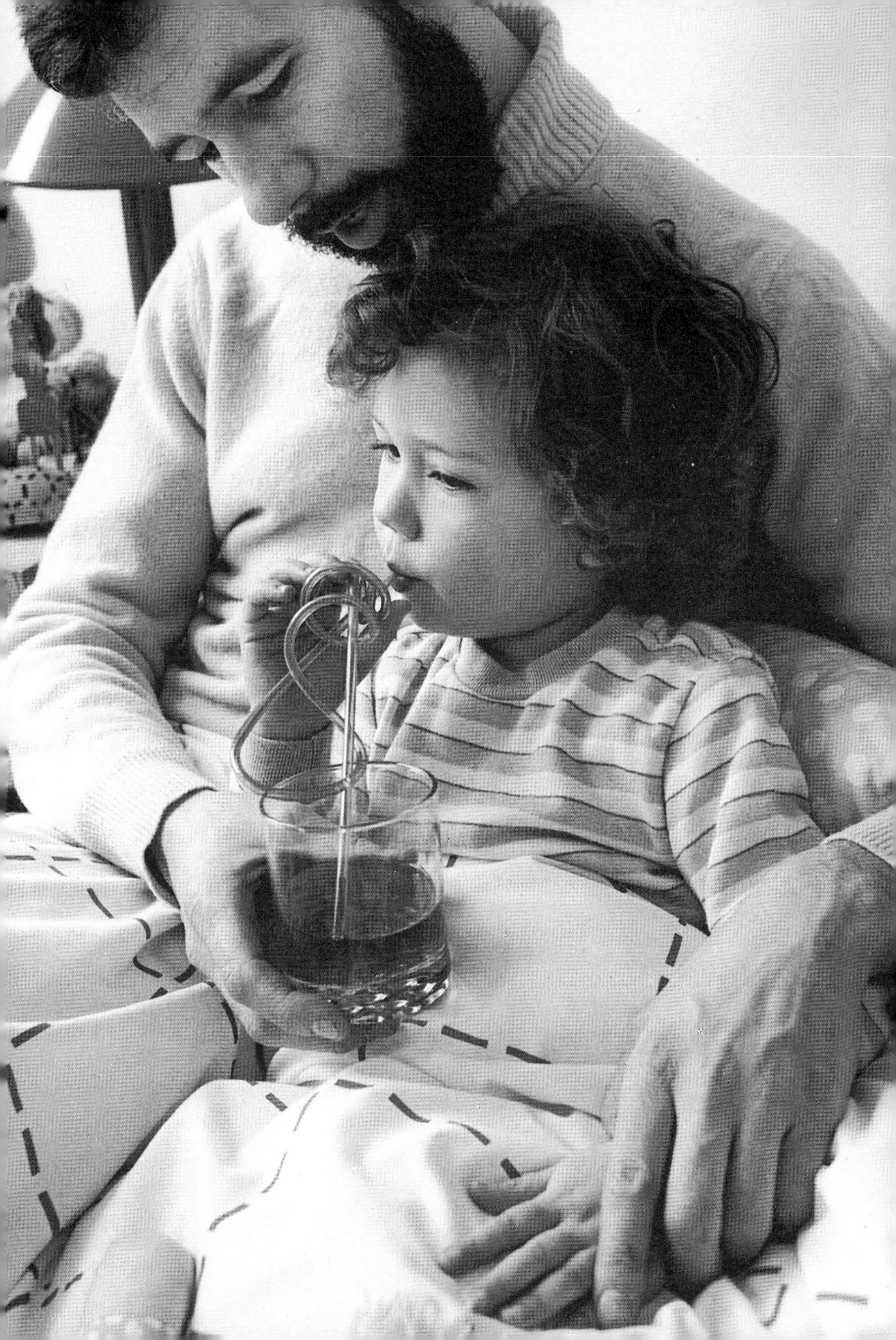

Fevers and infections

Fevers and infections such as influenza, tonsilitis, measles, chickenpox and mumps are the most common cause of appetite loss in young children and refusing food often occurs before other symptoms and can be very worrying.

The first dietary essential in these cases is to replace the fluid and salts lost through profuse sweating, vomiting and diarrhoea, in order to prevent dehydration. However, avoid giving sweetened drinks as these can cause stomach upsets. Bottled, low mineral, spring waters (still varieties only for young babies), unsalted vegetable stock made from green, leafy vegetables – carrots, leeks and onions – kombu seaweed stock, mixed lacto-fermented vegetable juice (diluted and given warm or unheated), very diluted, unsweetened fruit juices – apple, blackcurrant, lemon barley (home-made) – roasted brown rice tea or Japanese twig tea, are all suitable drinks.

Food for a sick child

As the appetite returns gradually introduce solids, as in the early stages of weaning, using vegetable purée soups, cereal gruels, fish and chicken stock soups or savoury egg custard. In cases of persistant diarrhoea (sometimes the result of overeating fruit or sweet foods but may also be caused by an infection) check with your doctor to establish the cause and if the appetite is good give brown rice as part of a savoury meal – the high fibre content helps absorb some of the excess fluid and reduce diarrhoea. If food is rejected give teaspoon amounts of fresh, finely grated apple or sips of freshly pressed, unsweetened apple juice, choosing low acid, sweet apples preferably organically grown, where possible. Sips of carrot juice or sieved carrot soup can also be effective and vegetable stock or apple juice thickened with arrowroot or kuzu has a gentle, settling effect on the digestion. Symptoms such as diarrhoea and vomiting are part of the body's defence mechanism and should not simply be repressed by medication as they may be indicative of a more deep-rooted problem. Take extra care with the general diet, eliminating sweets and refined, processed foods to prevent further occurrance of symptoms.

In an emergency, go straight to the casualty department of your local hospital and if you do not have a car, dial 999 for an ambulance. If possible telephone your doctor and tell him what has happened and where you are going. Being prepared in an emergency saves valuable time so it is wise to check what hospital facilities are available in your area and keep the day and a night number of your doctor by the telephone. Although you will not wish to pester your doctor unnecessarily neither can you be expected to know how potentially serious a change in your child's health could be, so if in doubt, ring him.

Health hazards

The children of parents who smoke are inevitably more prone to throat and lung problems such as coughs, bronchitis and pneumonia while damp housing, inner city pollution and pesticide sprayed fields create environmental health hazards for both adults and children that cannot always be so easily avoided. As a result of improved hygiene, nutrition and immunization, serious illness in children is less common than in the past yet, over the past forty or fifty years, other changes have taken place which have increased the incidence among children of certain degenerative diseases previously associated with later life – heart disease, cancer, rheumatoid arthritis. Dependence on a refined diet has been associated with these health problems and certainly many of the foods which our grandparents ate were radically different from their present day equivalents. Bread, whatever the colour, is likely to contain significantly higher amounts of artificial fertilizer and pesticide residue; sugar in its pure, refined form, contains no vitamins, minerals or trace elements but does contain traces of the chemicals used during the refining process; meats, dairy produce and eggs, contain higher levels of antibiotics, hormones and preservatives than previously and fruits and vegetables are subjected to intensive farming methods.

Additives to avoid

The following common food additives have been found to produce adverse symptoms in certain children and adults.

Colourings:

- E102 Tartrazine
- E110 Sunset Yellow FCF or Orange Yellow S
- E122 Carmoisine or Azorubine
- E123 Amaranth
- E124 Ponceau 4R or Cochineal Red A
- E127 Erythrosine BS

Preservatives:

- E211 Sodium benzoate
- E212 Potassium benzoate
- E214 Ethyl 4-hydroxybenzoate
- E215 Ethyl 4-hydroxybenzoate sodium salt
- E219 Methyl 4-hydroxybenzoate sodium salt
- E220 Sulphur dioxide
- E223 Sodium metabisulphite

Antioxidants:

- E320 Butylated hydroxyanisole
- E321 Butylated hydroxytoluene

Hyperactivity

Children with behavioural disorders often have physical problems such as hayfever, asthma, headaches and abdominal complaints. Symptoms are often triggered off by the foods they crave such as sugar, orange juice and packet foods containing additives or conversely by the foods they dislike – some children who won't drink milk eat large amounts of cheese.

Tartrazine, an orange colouring of the azo group listed above, is found in products such as orange squash, children's sweets and certain medications. It has been implicated as one of the substances which can trigger hyperactivity in children who exhibit this distressing condition. Children so labelled (and care should be taken before pinning a diagnostic tag on anyone) leave you in no doubt that they have a behavioural problem. They are more than simply over-boisterous – they seem at times unable to sit still or concentrate on any one occupation or event going on around them for more than a minute. They are often labelled troublesome, naughty or difficult at school or anywhere that they have to conform to a set pattern of behaviour. Generally highly intelligent, they often appear at odds with themselves as well as the rest of the world. Parents recognize that their 'hyperactive' children have two very distinct personalities: the quiet, thoughtful, bright and happy child and the irritable, sometimes aggressive, withdrawn child who appears to have little control over his actions.

The cause of hyperactivity is still disputed and although dietary exclusions of specific foods and the additives listed have proved successful in many cases further investigation into the role of diet and environmental pollutants is needed.

Diet for hyperactive children

The diet advocated by the late Dr Benjamin Feingold eliminates all processed foods containing artificial colourings, flavourings and preservatives, refined sugar foods and drinks and also, in the initial stages of treatment, the fruits and vegetables which contain the substance, salicylate, also found in aspirin. Many parents have found that their children's behaviour has improved on this diet but exclusions alone are not the total answer because, as previously mentioned, the long-term exclusion of major nutrient sources can create its own health problems. A diet based on fresh wholefoods including seasonal fruits and vegetables should be aimed at, both to prevent and enhance the cure of a condition such as hyperactivity. If, however, a child has had a behavioural disorder for some time there will be some acquired bad habits and a child psychiatrist is the person best qualified to give proper guidance at this stage. Some parents have reported that one of the first signs of improvement in their hyperactive child occurs when he realizes, for the first time, how disruptive his behaviour is.

Support groups

Support groups for parents with hyperactive children have been set up to give practical help and advice, consult Useful addresses (see page 124). Care should be taken not to self-treat or self-diagnose a child that has not been fully investigated by a doctor or specialist. However, parents can feed their children the kind of nutritious diet outlined in this book and know this will give them a solid basis for health.

Obesity

Chubby babies may look sweet but fat children stand out uncomfortably in a crowd. They are often excluded from games and activities such as team sports and swimming because they are clumsy or have less energy than thinner children. They may develop a poor, self-image because of being called 'tubby', 'fatty', or 'greedy', yet in reality the overweight child may not be eating any more food than his slimmer friends but he may be less active and his body may need fewer calories than his appetite demands.

If this results in excess weight it will be difficult to lose if a change in eating habits is not made. Factors which contribute to overweight in babies and children include the early introduction of solids, proprietary baby foods containing starch fillers, excessive bottlefeeding and decreased physical activity through use of cars and pushchairs. The overweight baby can easily become the overweight child. However, there is often a reduction in appetite between the ages of 2 and 4 and this, combined with upward growth spurts, usually means that by the time the child is 5 or 6 years old he is no longer plump. Studies investigating links between obesity in adults and birth weight have shown that in fact most overweight babies are within the normal range by the age of 7 and did not show an increased tendency to overweight in adulthood; whereas those who were overweight between the ages of 7 and 14 tended to remain overweight for the rest of their lives and were more prone to suffer from associated health risks such as diabetes and coronary heart disease.

SUGGESTED DAY'S MENU FOR AN OVERWEIGHT CHILD

Breakfast
Bowl of porridge or muesli with a dessertspoonful of soaked dried fruit to sweeten in place of sugar
Cup of milk or half a small tub of natural yoghurt

Mid-morning snack
Portion fresh fruit – pear, apple or 6 to 8 grapes

Lunch
Slice of roast chicken with blackcurrant jelly salad and shredded Chinese leaves or crispy lettuce (home-grown)
Sesame millet squares

Mid-afternoon snack
Chunky slice of rye bread with sunflower spread, served with a bowl of crunchy coleslaw salad (home-made)

Evening meal
Bowl of vegetable soup
Buckwheat noodles and lentil bolognese
Steamed broccoli

Evening snack
(at least two hours before bedtime)
Small glass unsweetened apple juice diluted with hot water
1–2 basic biscuits (omit sugar and add sesame seeds)

Restricting a child's food intake is difficult if parents and other children have large appetites but no weight problem so family co-operation is essential to ensure success. It is unfair to expect a child to sit through a meal comprising foods he is not supposed to eat. A healthy, reducing plan need not and should not leave the person feeling hungry or lacking in energy. On the contrary, wholegrain cereals, seasonal salads, lean meats and fish, nuts, seeds, fruit and low sugar biscuits will increase vitality, turn flab into muscle and fatness into fitness.

Hints to cut calories

□ Always check with your doctor before making any major dietary changes.
□ Treat milk as a food rather than a drink. For children over 5 years include fresh, low fat milk, yoghurts and cheeses. These provide the same protein and calcium as whole milk but lack the fat-soluble vitamins A and D – be sure to supply these in other foods (check Nutrient chart page 16). Skimmed milk and skimmed milk products should not be used for children under 2 years.
□ Increase fibre in the diet by using only 100% wholegrain flours and breads, breakfast cereals, pasta and savoury wholegrain dishes. High fibre foods are more filling than refined starch products.
□ Meal-in-a-bowl soups comprising wholegrains, vegetables, pulses and meat or fish make a filling lunch served with salad.
□ Fresh and dried fruits, nuts and seeds are better snacks than crisps or chocolate bars but snack eating of all kinds should be discouraged by giving satisfying main meals.
□ Avoid fried and fatty foods (such as sausages and hamburgers) unless home-made using low fat ingredients.
□ Keep main meals to two courses and only have a dessert as a special treat at week-ends.
□ Ask friends and relatives not to give sweets, fattening foods and drinks as presents.
□ Use diluted, unsweetened, fresh fruit juices to re-educate the taste buds to liking less sweet tastes. Tinned fruit in unsweetened juice, low sugar and no-sugar jams (not diabetic brands which contain high calorie Sorbitol), carob chocolate and carob powder are better choices for a sweet taste.
□ Salad vegetables, shredded, diced and sliced in appealing shapes (see page 121) make the food attractive and increase the need to chew which improves digestion.
□ Chewing slowly helps limit the amount of food eaten.
□ Drinking between rather than with meals prevents food being 'washed down' – another habit that can increase the volume of food eaten.

If your child has a dietary problem encourage participation in any special cooking preparation

☐ Using smaller plates is one way to give less without it seeming so obvious – serving the meal in a variety of small dishes, with contrasting colour and texture will all help to re-train attitudes to food, which is so often looked upon as a mere filler.
☐ Involve an older child in shopping and cooking to gain their interest and support, whether it is he who has the weight problem or another member of the family.
☐ Encourage older children to spend their pocket money on non-food items such as games, books or hobbies and if they do want snacks suggest fresh fruit, nuts, seeds or 'muesli bars' rather than poor quality sweets and flavoured crisps.

Overweight and the handicapped

There is an increased risk of overfeeding physically or mentally handicapped children. The desire to give pleasure through food or the belief that it is necessary to 'feed up' a previously sickly child is understandable but overweight can be a further handicap and increase proneness to other health problems so that you are literally adding to the burden of those looking after them. On the other hand, good nutrition may play an important part in improving the general health of such children and benefit their mental and physical development.

Coeliac disease

Coeliac disease is a condition in which there is a sensitivity to gluten, the protein found in wheat rye, barley and oats. Gluten gives the elasticity and binding capacity to these grains so expertly used by cooks to produce breads, cakes, sauces and soufflés. Of the grains which contain gluten wheat contains the most and oats and barley the least, hence some people diagnosed as Coeliac are able to tolerate small amounts of barley and oats. In Coeliac disease the lining of the small intestine becomes swollen and there is a loss of surface area of the digestive tract which upsets the digestion and absorption of fats and other nutrients. The result is a child with a wasted appearance and distended abdomen who produces bulky, frothy, fatty, foul-smelling stools.

A gluten-free diet is usually the sole treatment for this condition and generally the results are good provided the diet is strictly followed. The first signs of the condition show shortly after the foods containing gluten are introduced to the diet during weaning. The composition of the normal stools becomes bulky and offensive and gradually there is a loss of weight on the buttocks, arms and thighs and the child becomes irritable and often loses his appetite. As yet it is not clearly established whether the proneness to Coeliac disease is inherited or acquired which is why parents are advised to delay giving anything containing gluten until the baby is at least 4 months old and preferably not until after 6 months.

A gluten-free diet

This symbol on a label guarantees gluten-free contents

If your child is prescribed a gluten-free diet the doctor will refer you to a dietitian who will give you comprehensive advice on how to plan a nutritious, gluten-free diet.

Most recipes can be adapted for gluten-free use. Sauces can be thickened with arrowroot or kuzu and consult the recipe index for home-made fish fingers, hamburgers, meat loaves and baking using alternative, gluten-free flours. Commercially produced, gluten-free flours and products are available made from wheat starch but some people prefer to use foods which are naturally gluten-free such as brown rice, millet, maize (corn), potato, sago and bean flours such as soya and gram (chickpea).

When eating out choose fresh foods and plain meat or fish dishes without sauces. Fried potatoes may have been cooked in the same oil as battered or breaded foods and so will carry traces of gluten which could cause upsets. Take suitable breads, biscuits and breakfast cereals on holiday or when travelling.

If you have more than one child it is easier to prepare all main meals using gluten-free products. You are not depriving your other children who will eat foods containing gluten outside the home.

GLUTEN-FREE MENU FOR CHILD 1–2 YEARS

	BREAKFAST	LUNCH	EVENING MEAL
1	Brown rice porridge with soaked sultanas and sesame seed meal Milk	Shepherd's pie with minced beef, lamb or chicken, carrots and Brussels sprouts	Cottage cheese, apple and finely grated carrot salad on brown rice cakes
2	Scrambled egg and potato pizza base	Poached fish, vegetables and boiled potato	Brown rice pudding with sultanas (no added sugar)
3	Basic millet with apricot purée and sunflower seed meal	Slice meat loaf (using brown rice in place of breadcrumbs) and salad	Maize muffins and home-made apple sauce
4	Fresh fruit salad and natural yoghurt	Lentil and vegetable broth with brown rice in place of barley Puffed brown rice cake and sesame seed spread	Chicken cheese bake
5	Brown rice and ground almond porridge with milk	Grilled fish with banana and lemon juice stuffing	Chicken soup with brown rice and vegetables Savoury egg custard
6	Potato cheese cake (mashed potato and grated cheese baked or grilled)	Sweet and sour liver, seasonal salad and jacket potato	Fish soup with rice or potato noodles and vegetables – serve as a meal in a bowl with not too much broth
7	Puffed brown rice, puffed millet or puffed corn cereal with toasted seed meal and raisins	Sardine crisp Cup of clear soup	Family favourite big bean stew with millet balls (cook millet and bind with egg, roll in sesame seed meal and bake on top of casserole)

FOODS TO AVOID (which may contain gluten)

- ☐ Processed meats and cheeses, stock cubes, suet
- ☐ Breaded foods, pie fillings
- ☐ Tinned and packet soups and foods
- ☐ Mayonnaise, salad cream, sauces
- ☐ Baby foods, rusks
- ☐ Nut butters, lemon curd
- ☐ Powdered spices, pickles
- ☐ Sweets, drinks, chocolate
- ☐ Baking powder, flour, cornflour
- ☐ Wheat, wheat flour
- ☐ Wheat starch and protein
- ☐ Wholewheat, wholegrains
- ☐ Wholemeal, wheatgerm, bran
- ☐ Starch, thickening, cereal
- ☐ Rye, rye flour, pot barley
- ☐ Barley, barley meal
- ☐ Oats, oat flour, oatgerm
- ☐ Oatbran, oatmeal
- ☐ Monosodium glutamate
- ☐ Hydrolysed vegetable protein.

Diabetes mellitus

Diabetes mellitus is a condition in which the body is unable to make use of carbohydrates (starches and sugars) for energy production because of the lack of or reduced effectiveness of the hormone insulin which is supplied by the pancreas. Under normal circumstances, insulin is produced as and when required to transport the glucose in the bloodstream into the body cells where it is the main energy source for muscle and brain activity. When there is a lack of insulin the glucose builds up in the bloodstream until a limit is reached and glucose becomes detectable in the urine. Increased thirst and a pattern of excess drinking and urination are often the first signs of diabetes. Other symptoms include loss of weight, tiredness and apathy.

Diabetes mellitus is one of the most common of the endocrine disorders and most diabetics live normal, active lives. There is more of a tendency for children with one or both parents who are diabetic to develop diabetes themselves than for those with no family history of the disorder. An increasing trend for diabetics to be encouraged to follow diets based on high fibre wholegrains, fresh fruits and vegetables and low fat foods has proved beneficial for general health as well as control of the diabetes.

Insulin

Most children and young adults require insulin injections to control their condition. It is not possible to give insulin in tablet form as it is a protein and would be inactivated by digestion. The type of insulin prescribed by the doctor and the number of injections to be taken daily depend on individual circumstances such as age and activity and careful early instruction by doctor, nurse or parent usually eliminates any fears. Many young children are proficient at measuring their insulin dosage and giving themselves injections and this is to be encouraged (with appropriate supervision) to allow for independence and self-confidence as the child grows older and takes part in school and social activities away from home. Parents are advised not to become over-protective as the diabetic child should not be treated as an invalid nor told that he has a disease.

Diabetic diet

The quantity and type of carbohydrate in the diet of the diabetic is particularly important and regular mealtimes are necessary to coincide with the availability of insulin also given at regular intervals, either two or three times a day. Initially, careful weighing of food may be advised and lists of specific amounts of foods are given which contain the same amount of carbohydrate so that one can be exchanged for another to give a varied diet.

The aim of treatment is to provide sufficient insulin to keep blood levels of glucose within the normal range. The amount of

If your child has a dietary problem a dietitian will answer all your questions, give expert advice on diet and monitor his progress carefully

carbohydrate required is calculated to provide sufficient glucose in the blood during the times that the insulin is present in peak amounts. Diets which are high in fats and excess calories can lead to an increase in weight which is potentially harmful to the diabetic.

Tips for diabetics

□ Diabetics who take insulin (some older people with late onset diabetes can control the condition by diet alone) should always carry some form of quickly absorbable carbohydrate in case of an emergency – glucose tablets, barley sugar sweets, fruit juice are all easy to take. A carbohydrate snack such as crispbread with peanut butter, a piece of fresh fruit or a sandwich is worth carrying when away from home in case of a delayed meal or unexpected activity. Exercise has the effect of lowering blood sugar levels and this must be taken into consideration when planning diets for children who have increased energy demands at school on sports days.

□ Diabetics should always carry a card detailing their name, address, telephone number, doctor's telephone number, their insulin type and dosage and information about their diet and emergency foods.

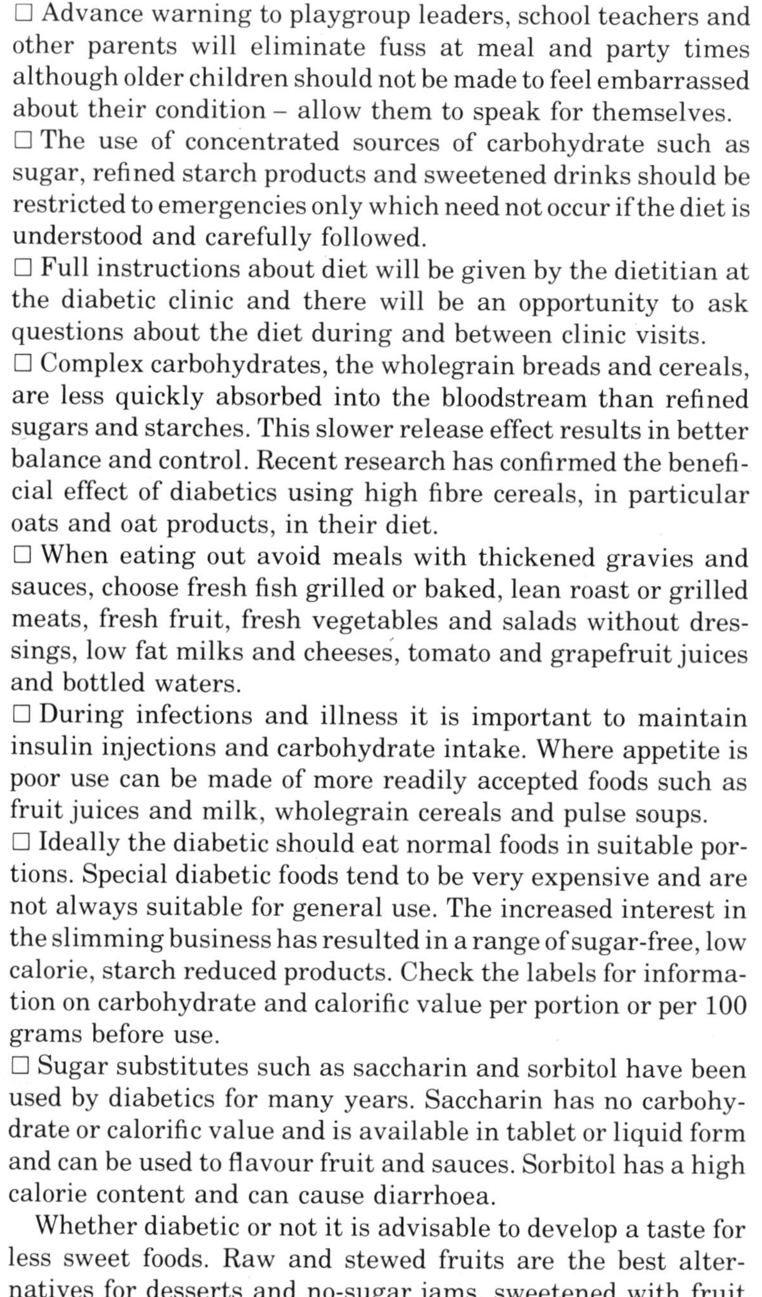

□ Advance warning to playgroup leaders, school teachers and other parents will eliminate fuss at meal and party times although older children should not be made to feel embarrassed about their condition – allow them to speak for themselves.

□ The use of concentrated sources of carbohydrate such as sugar, refined starch products and sweetened drinks should be restricted to emergencies only which need not occur if the diet is understood and carefully followed.

□ Full instructions about diet will be given by the dietitian at the diabetic clinic and there will be an opportunity to ask questions about the diet during and between clinic visits.

□ Complex carbohydrates, the wholegrain breads and cereals, are less quickly absorbed into the bloodstream than refined sugars and starches. This slower release effect results in better balance and control. Recent research has confirmed the beneficial effect of diabetics using high fibre cereals, in particular oats and oat products, in their diet.

□ When eating out avoid meals with thickened gravies and sauces, choose fresh fish grilled or baked, lean roast or grilled meats, fresh fruit, fresh vegetables and salads without dressings, low fat milks and cheeses, tomato and grapefruit juices and bottled waters.

□ During infections and illness it is important to maintain insulin injections and carbohydrate intake. Where appetite is poor use can be made of more readily accepted foods such as fruit juices and milk, wholegrain cereals and pulse soups.

□ Ideally the diabetic should eat normal foods in suitable portions. Special diabetic foods tend to be very expensive and are not always suitable for general use. The increased interest in the slimming business has resulted in a range of sugar-free, low calorie, starch reduced products. Check the labels for information on carbohydrate and calorific value per portion or per 100 grams before use.

□ Sugar substitutes such as saccharin and sorbitol have been used by diabetics for many years. Saccharin has no carbohydrate or calorific value and is available in tablet or liquid form and can be used to flavour fruit and sauces. Sorbitol has a high calorie content and can cause diarrhoea.

Whether diabetic or not it is advisable to develop a taste for less sweet foods. Raw and stewed fruits are the best alternatives for desserts and no-sugar jams, sweetened with fruit juice, are more flavourful than diabetic varieties flavoured with artificial sweeteners.

A list of carbohydrate values for proprietary products and other advice may be obtained from the British Diabetic Association (see page 124 for address).

Warn playgroup leaders, teachers and friends' parents if your child has a dietary problem, to minimize any possible fuss, but also encourage him to speak up for himself

Allergies and food intolerance

The term 'allergy' describes the protective mechanism used by the body when challenged by a foreign substance. As with infection the reaction may be local or general. In theory one could be allergic to almost any substance with which the body comes into contact. The commonest substances include milk, soya milk, cheese, eggs (especially egg white), fish (particularly shellfish), wheat, pork, peanuts, brewer's yeast, tomatoes, citrus fruits, strawberries, house dust mite, animal hair or dander, feathers and pollen. Reactions vary in severity, ranging from a localized rash to the streaming nose and eyes of hayfever, the wheezing lungs of asthma and the flaking skin of eczema. Symptoms of an upset digestion are also common – distended abdomen, gastritis and diarrhoea. In a true allergy there appears to be a hereditary factor – a child who has a parent with eczema or asthma may well show an allergic condition but not necessarily the same one as the parent and there is often a psychological factor with the allergy symptoms becoming more apparent in times of emotional stress.

Early weaning has been implicated as a possible cause of the increasing incidence of food allergy amongst infants and bottle-fed babies are more prone to allergy than breastfed babies, although cases of cow's milk sensitivity have been noted in breastfed babies whose mothers drink cow's milk. The gentle simmering of milk for 10 minutes will modify the protein in it, thus reducing the potentially harmful effect. Allergies in babies can manifest in a number of ways including gastric upsets, vomiting, diarrhoea, skin rashes, eczema, wheezing, asthma and lethargy and it is generally the protein factor in foods such as wheat gluten, milk, meat, fish and eggs which initiates the problem. The immature lining of the baby's digestive tract allows the passage of the large molecule proteins of the aforementioned foods into the bloodstream before they have been properly digested. They are then identified by the body as a threat to the system and antibodies are produced. Subsequent exposure to these foods results in the body reacting as if to an infection and repeated exposure results in a chronic ill-health condition which, if not identified as a food allergy, can have a long-term effect on the child's health. Careful introduction of foods during weaning has been shown to reduce the incidence of allergic reactions and makes the identification of problem foods easier.

Being aware that allergies exist means parents can note their child's reaction to any new food and seek advice if there appears to be any intolerance. But do not underestimate your powers of suggestion! Negative feelings can be communicated to your baby and if you fear that your child may be sensitive to a particular food they may live up to your expectations.

Eczema

There are many types of eczema, which is a non-infectious skin problem, and it has a variety of causes. In many cases the cause is an allergy to an environmental or food factor. Mothers sometimes observe that certain foods cause itching and remove these from the diet with success. On occasions so many foods seem to result in eczema that dietary restriction would mean nutrient deficiency. Most commonly implicated foods include milk and other dairy produce, eggs, wheat (especially commercial wheat), citrus fruits and tomatoes. No major nutrient source should be removed from the diet without professional guidance. The house dust mite has also been implicated and a doctor of homoeopathy should be consulted for advice on this matter.

It is important that adults with eczema and/or asthma (these two conditions plus food intolerance often appear together) review their health and diet prior to planning a family in order to reduce the risk of passing on the susceptibility to these conditions, to their children.

Specialist advice

Whatever the problem, do not put your child on a diet or impose any dietary restrictions without consulting your doctor who can refer you and your child to a dietitian for specialist advice if required.

Accidents

Children are naturally inquisitive so parents must anticipate dangers and remove them before accidents happen. Tablecloths, trailing flexes, frayed carpets, stairs, beds and chairs, pot handles, open fires, matches, hot irons, buttons, pins and bits of toys, knives, scissors and razor blades, colourful pills and poisonous liquids, alcohol and nail polish, plastic bags, slippery baths, tight clothes, pillows or the cat can all cause serious accidents if your child is not constantly watched. So make your home as safe as possible and be sure that you have enough rest and time to yourselves because overtiredness can lead to carelessness and inefficiency.

First-aid kit

Keep a simple first-aid kit in the car, the kitchen and the bathroom – easily accessible but out of reach of children. Replace any item as soon as it is used. Basics should include: assorted plasters, a small box of sterile gauze and cotton wool, 2 cotton bandages, 1 stretch bandage, scissors, safety pins, tweezers, paper tissues, homoeopathic urtica ointment for burns, homoeopathic hypercal ointment for soothing and healing cuts and abrasions, homoeopathic arnica tablets 6× potency for preventing and relieving muscle strain, bruising and concussion, homoeopathic aconite 6× in all cases of mental or physical shock, homoeopathic hypericum 6× for crushed finger tips, dog bites, thorn and nail wounds, homoeopathic nux vomica 6× potency, for gastric upset, particularly as a result of over-eating.

Choking

There is always a danger of choking on a food which has not been properly chewed or which is inhaled prior to chewing. Sieving and puréeing baby food is essential in the early stages but once finger feeding and self-feeding start and the food is less bland, the risk of choking is increased. Never leave a baby or young child alone with food. If a tiny baby chokes turn him upside down and hold him by his ankles. Pat his back between the shoulder blades to dislodge the foreign body from his windpipe. With an older baby or child, place him on his stomach, support his head and hold his nose so that the mouth opens. Pat sharply with the flat of the hand on the upper part of the back. If an object is blocking the windpipe, stand behind the child crossing your arms under his ribcage and jerk upwards to dislodge the object. If something sharp or rough is swallowed immediately feed with bread spread with jam or honey, mashed potato or a soft porridge and call the doctor.

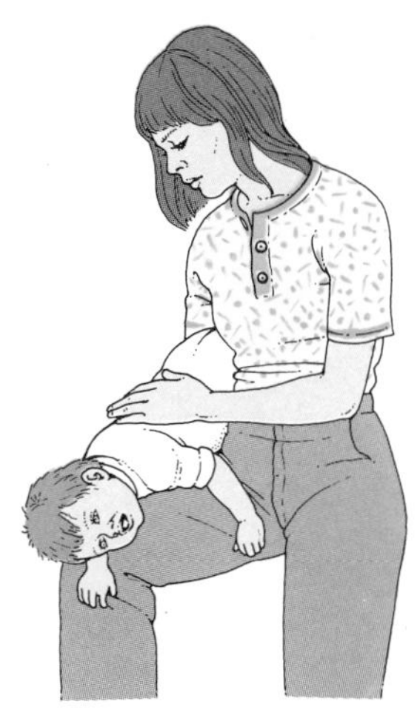

NB Items other than food can cause choking so keep small objects out of a baby's reach.

Appendix 1 GLOSSARY OF FOODS

Milk

The breast milk of a healthy mother will supply all the baby's food needs for the first 4 to 6 months of life and only specially formulated baby milks should be used as a substitute for breast milk. After this time supplements of other foods are necessary to meet the baby's increased needs for specific nutrients such as iron. With the introduction of other foods, breast and formula milk feeds are reduced. Cow's milk is not an essential food and is best not given unmodified, if used at all, before the baby is one year old. Goat's milk, available in both fresh and dried forms, is better tolerated in some cases than cow's milk and may be introduced at 10 months. If used earlier, goat's milk will require supplementation with folic acid and vitamin B12. Skimmed milk is lacking in the fat-soluble vitamins A and D and is therefore unsuitable as the main milk source for children under 5 years.

Water

Water filter

Drinking water should be pre-boiled until a baby is 10 months old and tap water can be tested for lead, copper and fluoride content by contacting your local water board. Soft water areas, where the water is low in calcium, tend to have higher levels of lead from lead pipes or copper from copper pipes in the water as a result of the higher acidity of the water which causes corrosion of water pipes. Jug style water filters can be bought which remove these whilst preventing bacterial contamination. A high lead content in the blood has been linked with poor brain development. Bottled spring water can be used but take care to choose one low in sodium and other minerals and avoid carbonated and distilled waters.

Juices

Start with pure carrot and apple juices. Choose varieties made from organically grown apples or vegetables that have been pulped and bottled without sugar, colouring or preservative or finely grate and squeeze pulp through muslin. Mix one part juice with ten parts water. Offer from a spoon, not a bottle, to test for tolerance. Gradually decrease dilution but be careful not to overfeed with juices which are a very concentrated form of nourishment. Apple juice is often less acidic and better tolerated than citrus juices. Many babies cannot tolerate orange juice which produces a rash or stomach upset. Also try grape and blackcurrant juices.

Other drinks

Most squashes and soft drinks contain additives, colouring and sugar or artificial sweetener so are best avoided. Tea and coffee are both high in the stimulant caffeine, which is unsuitable for children. Japanese twig tea or grain coffees make ideal, mild flavoured, non-stimulant drinks.

Fruit

Fruit should always be peeled (unless organically grown and guaranteed unsprayed). Fruit trees are surface feeders and even traces of weedkiller sprayed on surrounding grass can affect the fruit. Cooked fruit such as purées, spreads or agar agar jelly, is easier to digest than raw fruit. Pieces of apple and pear can be offered raw as finger foods. Apple is a tasty diversion rather than a real teething aid. Oranges and orange juice can produce skin-rashes and stomach upsets in young babies even though they often like them so introduce citrus fruit cautiously. Banana as a food for babies is a recent innovation and may not suit all, particularly in colder climates where tropical fruits are usually artificially ripened and more acid, so they are a less suitable choice than home-grown berries, apples and pears. If liked, bananas can be mashed with a little sesame seed meal for younger children or given in bite-sized pieces in place of sweets for older children. Always choose small bananas as they are usually sweeter and only use when fully ripened. The diluted juice of soaked dried fruits (unsulphured) can be given as a mild laxative and purée of soaked dried apricots or sultanas can be used as a natural sweetener (these are also a good source of iron). The natural fruit sugar, fructose, provides plenty of sweetness and combined with cellulose (fibre), vitamin and mineral elements, fruit is an excellent aid to the digestion.

Vegetables

These play an important part in the diet, providing essential vitamins, minerals, trace elements and natural fibre. In addition they add to the attractive appearance of a meal with varied colour, flavour, texture and aroma. *Bulbs, roots and tubers* – start with carrot then try turnip, swede, parsnip, leek, onion, radish (white daikon/mooli has a less peppery flavour) and potato. *Green vegetables and flower buds* – cauliflower, broccoli and Brussels sprouts make popular purées. Cabbage, spring greens and kale may cause digestive upsets if used in excess or not properly cooked. Puréed with a little wholegrain cereal these are often better tolerated. Spinach, high in oxalic acid, a substance which binds calcium, is best not fed to babies under one year. *Salad leaves* – lettuce is available in many varieties from large leaved and soft to small and crisp but, if possible, avoid commercial varieties that are highly sprayed during growth to prevent spoilage. Watercress, chicory, endive, and landcress can be served freshly shredded or as finger foods or used as a colourful garnish over a cooked dish. *Vegetable fruits and seeds* – always test cucumbers for flavour and avoid giving those with a bitter taste. Although generally used as a salad ingredient, diced cucumber is delicious when cooked. Summer and winter squash, marrow, pumpkin, sweetcorn, beans and peas, make good soups and stews but mushrooms do not always suit infant tastes. The smooth texture and buttery flavour of avocado is often well liked (see recipe for avocado spread). *Stems* – celery stalks make suitable finger foods and are often preferred raw. Asparagus are rare and expensive adult finger foods which infants might like to try! *Frozen vegetables* may retain their nutrients but they lose much of their flavour and lack the texture of fresh varieties. However, they are useful when fresh produce is hard to obtain. *Tinned vegetables* are pre-cooked, processed, and contain a selection of additives including artificial colouring, preservatives and salt. Most are unsuitable for babies. *Dried vegetables*, when rehydrated, give a useful and often flavoursome source of fibre but lack the vitamins found in fresh produce. *Tomatoes* – use with caution. These appear on most allergy lists and can cause digestive upsets in some people. However, when the skin and pips are removed a more digestible pulp is left which is best used in cooking rather than eaten raw. Commercially grown tomatoes tend to be heavily sprayed with pesticides but miniature varieties are easy to grow, even in a window-box, and produce sweet, low acid 'fruits'.

Growing your own fruit and vegetables by organic/bio-dynamic methods is becoming increasingly popular and for most people it is the only way to ensure a supply of freshly picked, unsprayed, well-flavoured produce. Easy to grow are bean and seed sprouts (see page 67). These can be added to bread, scone and batter recipes, bean and nut burgers.

Sea vegetables

Sea vegetables contain a wide range of minerals, trace elements and vitamins essential to the body. There are a variety of sea vegetables such as Irish dulse and carrageen, Japanese kombu (kelp), wakame, arame and nori (sea lettuce or Welsh laver). Many can be bought in health food shops in the dried form and can be relied upon for quality and cleanliness when bought pre-packed. They also have the advantage of being easily stored in an airtight container. It is of course possible to use fresh seaweed from the shores of our coastlines but when doing this be sure to choose a stretch of coast well away from possible contamination by sewage and chemical waste. Seaweed picked off the beach should never be used. Use only that which has been freshly harvested from the rocks at sea level.
Dulse – simply rinse a 5–10 cm (2–4 in) piece to re-hydrate and serve, finely sliced, in salad or added to soups and cooked vegetables. It is a wonderful source of iron.
Wakame – soak a 15 cm (6 in) piece of wakame in enough water to cover for 3 minutes. Remove stalk and keep for cooking with beans or adding to soup stock. Cut remainder into 2.5 cm (1 in) slices. Add to vegetable, bean and meat casseroles, soups and salads.
Nori – comes as flakes which

can be added to soups, sauces or casseroles, or as flat sheets. The sheets can be lightly toasted to crisp (it only takes seconds over a flame or under the grill). The colour will change from dark to light green. Break into 2.5 cm (1 in) squares and serve as crisps or slice into strips and use to wrap around brown rice which has been formed into balls. This looks very pretty when decorated with a carrot flower.
Arame – jet black and composed of very fine shreds it requires cooking before use but once cooked it can be used in casseroles, stews or salads.

Teething foods
Naturally hard foods, such as root vegetables, chunks of peeled cucumber, pear or apple are the best teething aids. They offer comfort and distraction when teething begins at about 6 months. Some babies suffer more discomfort than others but on the whole the better nourished the baby the less trouble there appears to be. Puffed rice cakes (made from gluten-free puffed brown rice and available salt-free) or home-made rusks are better than shop bought varieties which contain sugar.

Meat
When choosing meat go for quality rather than quantity. Free-range poultry, and hill-fed lamb and beef are preferable to the meat of intensively-reared animals. Avoid all tinned meats, pork and its products, bacon, ham, gammon, luncheon meat, patés and sausages. All are high in fat and additives, including nitrates, which have been linked with cancer.

Fish
Fresh fish has been an important food in the diets of many races renowned for good health. Fish oils are a rich source of the fat-soluble vitamins essential for the proper development of bones and teeth and the health of eyes and skin. Always take care to remove all bones before serving and avoid tinned, smoked and processed frozen fish. Allergies to shellfish can occur so these are best introduced from the second year. White fish is easier to digest than oily fish. Although good quality fish can be an expensive item, it is quick to cook and has little waste. Serve with vegetables and grains but avoid serving with pulses as this can cause indigestion in some people. Herbs such as fennel, dill and caraway seed enhance the flavour and digestibility of fish.

Yoghurt
This is easily made in the home using cow's milk or goat's milk. A variety of gadgets and machines are available but the simplest is the wide-necked flask and thermometer. Always make sure utensils are scrupulously clean. Beneficial bacteria in yoghurt are added to warm milk and the resulting produce is both easier to digest than milk and rich in vitamins. Cow's or goat's milk yoghurt is suitable from 10 months and are available in many supermarkets in natural and sweetened form. Always buy the natural form and check for additives. If buying goat's milk yoghurt always check the source to make sure that the animals have a clean bill of health.

Tofu
A traditional Oriental food, tofu is produced from the soya bean by a method resembling cheese-making. White and smooth textured, tofu has a bland, slightly beany taste. It is an ideal way of fortifying favourite foods with extra protein and calcium. Low in fat it is easy to digest and as it lacks a distinct flavour tofu takes on the taste of the food with which it is cooked or combined. Commercially available, tofu is pre-cooked and can be used in dips and spreads. Unprocessed soya beans should never be eaten raw.

Cheese
Curd or cottage cheese can be made in the home using cow's milk or goat's milk. Easier to digest than hard cheeses they also have the advantage of being made without salt. Shop-bought cheeses including cottage cheese have added salt and these should be used sparingly for the first 2 years. White cheeses are preferable to artificially-coloured cheese. Small amounts, finely grated, add to a dish's nutritional value.

Eggs
Eggs come high on allergy lists, in particular egg white. Egg yolk, hard boiled, is best offered first to test for sensitivity. Free-range eggs are preferred for flavour and may have a lower allergy risk. A concentrated nutrient source, eggs are best used sparingly in infant diets. Do not offer egg white or whole egg under 18 months and not at all unless egg yolk is well tolerated, especially if the father or mother has had an eczema or asthma problem.

Nuts and seeds

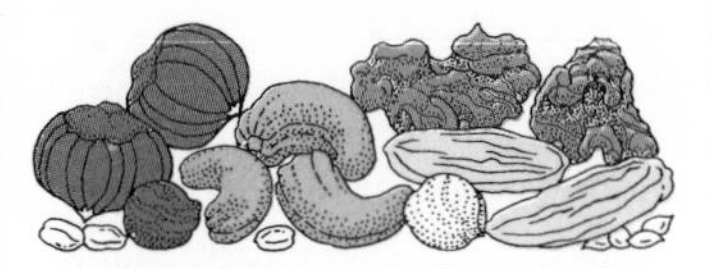

Salted and roasted varieties should never be used. Whole nuts are indigestible and dangerous if swallowed as they could cause a blockage in the windpipe, but finely ground and made into nut milks, creams and spreads they are a nourishing food high in protein, vitamins and minerals. Light toasting brings out the flavour and improves digestibility. Peanuts are, in fact, raw beans and so best avoided for babies unless cooked. The best nuts to use are almonds, hazelnuts, walnuts and cashews; the best seeds include sesame seeds, tahini (made from crushed sesame seeds – use the light, dehusked variety for infants), sunflower seeds, pumpkin seeds and pine kernels. Always buy nuts and seeds as fresh as possible because they are high in oil and become rancid with age. Store in an airtight container in a cool place.

Pulses

This is a collective term for dried peas, beans and lentils also known as legumes. Combined with wholegrain cereals, nuts or seeds, pulses provide complete protein. Economical, nourishing and tasty they are an ideal food for growing families. See Appendix 3 for standard cooking instructions. Split peas and the smaller beans and lentils combine well with vegetables to make purée soups suitable as weaning foods. Larger, cooked beans make good finger foods and when sprouted, pulses are a low calorie, high protein, vitamin- and mineral-rich snack, salad or stir-fry ingredient. Never give pulses raw, prior to sprouting, and always boil beans for at least ten minutes before reducing heat to complete cooking. Sprouting and boiling inactivate the substance which inhibits the proper digestion of protein and can cause digestive upsets. Pulses combine well with grains, vegetables, nuts, seeds and meats but not generally with fish or shellfish.

Cereals/grains

Wholegrain cereals combined with pulses, nuts, seeds or milk, cheese or yoghurt, constitute complete protein and so are particularly useful for non-meat eaters. Choose organically grown grains whenever possible to reduce exposure to residues of potentially harmful pesticides and artificial fertilizers. Brown rice and millet are gluten-free and easy to digest. Using whole rather than refined grains ensures the best vitamin and mineral content and a natural source of dietary fibre. Barley, oats and rye flakes combine well with brown rice as a breakfast cereal, or they can be used in soups and casseroles. Rye is believed to supply nutrients which are protective to the tooth enamel. Wheat, high in gluten (the protein part of the grain), is less easy to digest than other grains. Do not use wheat in any form before 8 months, then use organically grown wheat only (see wheat list for foods to avoid containing commercial wheat). Buckwheat is, in fact, a seed and not a grain. For babies it is best used as noodles, available with and without wheat. Corn or maize is gluten-free, but some babies are sensitive to it epecially in the flour form. The term cereals is used throughout this book to mean wholegrain cereals and not the highly processed, package varieties. See Appendix 3 Cooking techniques for standard cooking instructions.

Bread

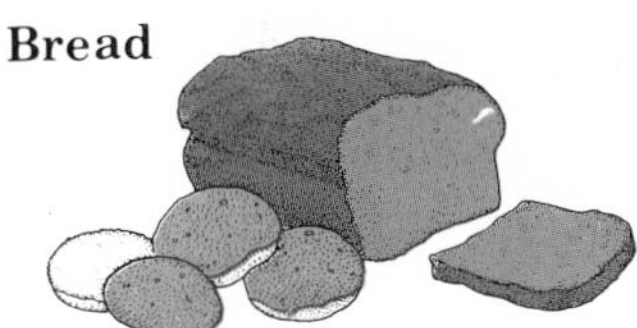

Home-made, mixed grain or organically grown wholewheat bread is advised here to avoid the possible sensitivity to additives used in commercial bread or to chemicals used in the non-organic farming of wheat. High in the protein factor gluten, wheat must be avoided by all those who are gluten sensitive (Coeliac). Rye, barley, and oats may also have to be avoided. Recipes are included giving gluten-free alternatives to regular flours. Because of its high gluten content wheat makes the best textured bread. Rye, barley and oats contain decreasing amounts of gluten and rice, millet and maize are gluten-free. For best flavours and nourishment a mixture of grain flours can be used: 25 per cent rye or barley plus 75 per cent organic wholewheat is a good combination. Nut and seed meals, sprouted grains and pulses are additions which make appetizing loaves.

Pasta

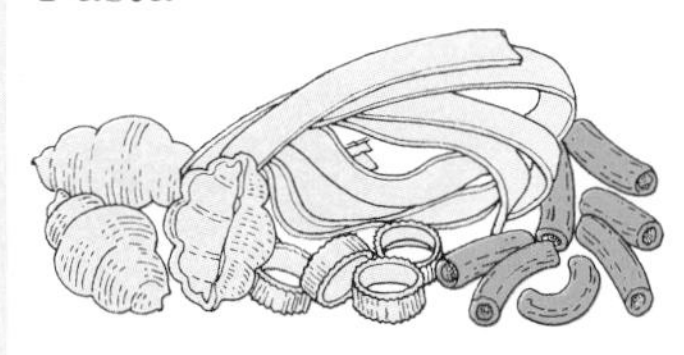

Under 12 months the use of 100 per cent buckwheat, soba noodles is advised as they are preferable to wheat pasta. Unless making your own with organically grown wholewheat flour, pasta is best avoided for children under 2 years. Refined white flour pasta is potentially fattening especially when served with a cheese sauce.

Biscuits and cakes

Under 2 years such foods are an unnecessary addition which can spoil the child's appetite for real foods. It is possible to make cakes and biscuits more wholesome by using the best quality ingredients, carefully chosen to suit your child's needs. Gluten-free recipes are included which can be used by the whole family. Home-made, low sugar equivalents to shop-bought cakes and biscuits are full of flavour and nourishment and soon become favourites.

Fibre
Fibre is an essential ingredient in the daily diet for proper digestion and elimination. Fibre adds bulk making wholefoods more filling and satisfying and it is ideal for slimmers and those with voracious appetites. Sources of fibre include wholegrain cereals, vegetables, pulses, fruit, nuts and seeds. Cereal fibre absorbs liquid during digestion easing the passage of food through the digestive system. However, following the scientific recognition of the need for fibre, bran has been 'prescribed' as a cure for constipation and diarrhoea but in some cases this can do more harm than good, particularly where there is a wheat sensitivity, as most brans are derived from wheat. Rice, oat and soya bran are available but should similarly be used with caution and are no replacement for fresh wholefoods. Bran is often sprinkled dry over food but, in fact, if used it should be incorporated into a dish such as porridge, soup or a casserole where it can absorb some fluid before being ingested. Similarly, wholegrain flour products are less effective as fibre sources than whole or flaked grains because the fine flour particles tend to dry during baking. A high fibre diet has been found beneficial in the management of diabetes mellitus (see page 104) and cereal fibre has also been shown to have a cholesterol binding effect of particular benefit to those with arteriosclerosis.

Oils
These are derived from seeds such as sunflower, sesame and maize, fruits such as the olive and pulses such as soya bean and peanut. The polyunsaturated fatty acids which they contain are thought preferable to the saturated fats found in animal fats and hardened vegetable fats. High temperatures change the structure of oil making it difficult to digest and a potential health-hazard. Babies and young children should not be fed deep-fried food. Gentle shallow frying or stir-frying is an appetizing way to cook vegetables. Always use low temperatures and the minimum of oil. Choose best quality, additive-free, cold pressed oils such as sunflower and maize for general purposes and sesame and olive for special occasions. Fish liver oils are a rich source of the fat-soluble vitamins A and D. These are available as drops or capsules and may be advised by your doctor.

Butter and Margarine
Fresh, unsalted butter is additive free and more beneficial than highly processed margarines. The quality of the milk used to make butter determines how nutritious it is and butter made from spring and summer herds is a good source of the fat-soluble vitamins A and D. Sparing use should be made of all oils and fats in the diet.

Sweet treats
Shop-bought sweets are high in refined sugar, artificial colourings and flavourings so their consumption should be kept to a minimum. The orange colouring tartrazine (E102) used in orange squash has been implicated as triggering behavioural disorders in children suffering from hyperactivity (see page 97). Recipes are included for alternative, low sugar sweet treats based on fruits, nuts and seeds.

Honey
Unpasteurized honey is not advised for babies under one year because of a rare but possible risk of infant botulism; a form of food poisoning which can be fatal to tiny babies. The occasional, sparing use of a good quality, pasteurized honey is suitable from 10 months.

Sweeteners
There are many alternatives to refined sugar which offer more than simply sweetness but all sweeteners should be used sparingly. Babies and children often have a preference for sweet tastes but this is not an indication of a need for sugar. Sweet alternatives include fresh, raw and cooked seasonal fruits and dried fruits, carefully cooked root vegetables, grain syrups, brown rice and barley malt, maple syrup, concentrated unsweetened fruit juices and carob. Carob powder is the flour of the carob bean which is naturally sweet and has a chocolate flavour. Free from the stimulant factor found in chocolate it can be used in place of chocolate in drinks. Unrefined sugars, such as muscovado and barbados, contain traces of vitamins and minerals. Blackstrap molasses is a useful source of iron. All have a laxative effect. This and their comparatively high cost suggests restricted use! It is tempting for parents of children with small appetites to feed them something sweet if they obviously relish it but the results of this indulgence in the long-term cannot be overlooked: paleness, susceptibility to infection, inferior bone growth, tooth and blood formation. Once parents give up the sugar habit themselves they find it easier to prevent the introduction of sugar and sugary foods and drinks into their children's diet.

Seasonings
There is no need to add salt to salads or carefully cooked vegetables. Those who never acquire the salt habit enjoy the wide variety of subtle flavours fresh foods have to offer. Excessive addition of salt at any age is harmful but particularly so in infancy. Sea salt has a better balance of minerals and is additive-free (unlike table salt which can contain aluminium to enable free-flow from the salt-cellar) but it is still salt and should not be used for children under 18 months to 2 years and then only in strict moderation when cooking grains. All salted foods should be avoided until this time. The use of fresh and dried herbs and well-flavoured vegetables of the onion family make up for the non-addition of salt. Spices such as curry powder, nutmeg, mustard and pepper should not be used. *Gomasio (sesame salt)* is made by grinding together lightly roasted sesame seeds with roasted sea salt in the proportions of eighteen parts sesame seed to one part salt for children. A mineral-rich, lower salt version can be made using kelp powder or roasted seaweed in place of salt. Sprinkle a few grains over cooked porridge and other wholegrains to bring out the flavour. Use for children over 12 months. *Tamari* is a high quality, wheat-free, additive-free soya sauce made from fermented soya beans and sea salt only. Use sparingly from 18 months. *Shoyu* is a traditional soya sauce made by fermenting soya beans, sea salt and wheat for at least eighteen months. Although other soya sauces are available these generally contain colouring, artificial flavouring, sugar and preservative and are best avoided by adults and children. *Miso* is a traditional Oriental food made by fermenting soya beans with sea salt and grain. The process takes about two years to complete and the finished product is a richly flavoured, dark paste which can be used as a savoury stock in soups and casseroles in place of bone stock or stock cubes. Miso contains live enzymes which aid digestion; protein in the form of easily assimilable amino acids; minerals such as calcium and iron; and vitamins including vitamin B12 not normally found in non-animal foods.

Nutritional or brewer's yeast
Available as a dried powder, brewer's yeast can be added as a protein, vitamin and mineral-rich addition to any soup, sauce or casserole. Introduce very gradually, using only half a teaspoon at first. It contains all the essential amino acids and B group vitamins including folic acid (deficient in goat's milk) and vitamin B12 (not normally found in non-animal foods). It also contains significant amounts of calcium, phosphorus and iron as well as the trace elements chromium and selenium.
NB Never use baker's yeast or any other form of live yeast in the uncooked form.

Vitamin and mineral supplements

Supplements are not generally required if the mother's diet has been good prior to and during breastfeeding and if the baby is weaned on to a diet of fresh wholefoods. Vitamin D is essential for the proper utilization of calcium required for the development of bones and teeth. Exposure to sunlight which triggers vitamin D production in the body via the skin is very important for children who do not eat animal foods. Mothers and children with dark skins may be at risk of low intake and advised to take supplements in countries with lower levels of sunlight. Fish liver oils and animal fats are the best sources of vitamin D although seaweeds also contain some. Vitamins A, D, and C are available as drops so ask your doctor or health visitor for advice on the need to use these in your particular case. As they are fat-soluble, vitamins A and D are stored in the body and there is a risk of overdosage if the recommended amount is exceeded. The fewer foods there are in the diet the greater the need for supplementation. Breast milk supplies all nutrients in the correct proportion for up to the first 6 months of life. Children who eat no animal foods (milk, cheese, eggs, fish or meat) will need a vitamin B12 supplement and a calcium supplement may also be needed unless adequate dehusked sesame seeds, pulses, almonds, leafy green vegetables and seaweeds are taken in the diet. Because milk is a poor source of iron it is necessary to bring in food sources containing this mineral early in weaning to prevent anaemia. Iron supplements are rarely prescribed. Useful amounts of iron can be obtained from wholegrain cereals, green leafy vegetables and dried fruits such as apricots. Red meat is generally regarded as the best source of iron but dulse is even better.

Commercial baby foods

There are times when commercial baby foods can be very useful, for example, when travelling or when fresh produce is not available. Choose jars rather than tins in case lead solder has been used to seal tin edges because seepage of lead into the food can occur. When buying jars of baby foods choose single item products for best value: plain fruit purées, vegetables or meats rather than combination 'meals' such as mixed dinners, fruit puddings and desserts. Always check ingredients lists and avoid foods containing sugar, colouring, artificial flavouring, salt, food starch or wheat. Do not feed directly from the jar unless your baby is taking the full jar of food at one feeding. Remove from the jar only the amount you expect to use, recover and use the remainder within two days. Store in original jar in the refrigerator and thoroughly heat before serving again. There is a risk that if you predominantly use commercial baby foods your child will develop a taste for these products, making a change to home-made, freshly prepared foods an added difficulty. It is best to keep commercial foods for emergency use only.

Foods containing wheat

Many packeted and tinned foods contain wheat so if wheat needs to be avoided read all food labels and check the ingredients listed. □ Most breads, buns, cookies, scones, pancakes, biscuits, cakes, pastries, certain oatcakes, non-rye crispbreads and rusks are made with, or include, wheat-refined or wholewheat-wheatgerm, bran □ Many breakfast cereals contain wheat, wheatgerm or bran including some muesli cereals, Weetabix and All Bran □ Most thickened soups, stews and gravies □ Processed and tinned meats such as corned beef, sausages, beef and hamburgers, salami, black pudding may contain cereal (wheat) and/or monosodium glutamate □ All foods containing monosodium glutamate □ All battered and breaded foods such as fish fingers, foods with flour-based sauces such as cauliflower cheese, white fish in parsley sauce, chicken supreme □ All products containing food starch or wheat starch such as salad cream, stock cubes, Bovril, ice-cream □ Some cornflours and custard powders and milk puddings □ Spaghetti, macaroni, pastas □ Bulghur (cracked wheat), couscous, spelt (ancient wheat) □ Mustard powder and some pastes. Wholegrain mustards do not contain flour □ Most chocolate and many other sweets □ Some instant coffees and malted drinks.

Appendix 2 PROTEIN COMPLEMENTATION

Protein in foods is broken down during digestion into amino acids which are then used as the basic building blocks of all body structures. There are twenty amino acids of which eight (ten for children) which are labelled 'essential' because they must be supplied in the diet and cannot be manufactured in the body like the remaining twelve (ten for children).

Complete and incomplete protein

A protein containing all eight essential amino acids is said to be *complete* and can be used to build and repair body tissues. Proteins which are partly or completely lacking in one or more essential amino acids are said to be *incomplete*. Except for soya beans, sesame seeds, almonds, yeast and wheatgerm most plant or vegetable proteins are regarded as incomplete but by combining two or more of these proteins of differing composition it is possible to make up any deficiency and such combinations of proteins are known as protein complementation.

Protein combinations

Economical use can be made of animal proteins by combining them with wholegrains, pulses, nuts, seeds, and vegetables. Lamb and bean hot-pot, roast chicken with oatmeal stuffing, kedgeree, are all examples of such combinations. Although research has shown that it is not absolutely necessary to combine all essential amino acids at one meal it makes sense to eat proteins which make an ideal combination together.

FOOD COMBINATIONS

Complete protein can be created by combining the following foods

Wholegrain cereals + pulses
Millet + aduki beans
Oats + brown lentils
Organic wholewheat bread + haricot beans
Brown rice + lentil bayleaf sauce
Barley broth + black-eye beans
Wholegrain and bean loaves
Sweetcorn and bean chowder

Wholegrain cereals + dairy products
Oat and dulse soup + natural yoghurt
Millet casserole + cheese crumble topping
Barley and rye flour crêpes + cottage cheese, spring onion and tomato filling
Cauliflower supreme + white cheese sauce
Cream of chicken and brown rice soup (with milk)
Brown rice, sultana and date milk pudding

Wholegrain cereals + nuts and seeds
(With the exception of sesame seeds or almonds + brown rice the addition of pulses or dairy produce is also required)
Brown rice balls + toasted sesame seed meal
Millet + cashew nuts + chickpeas
Brown rice breakfast dish + tahini
Mixed grain toast + tahini

Wholegrain cereals + brewer's yeast
Bean and vegetable hot-pot + brown rice

Seeds (sesame, sunflower, pumpkin) + pulses
Tahini and lentil spread
Bean loaf with added wholegrain and seeds
Hummus (chickpeas, onion, garlic and tahini)
Sautéd tofu + steamed broccoli on brown rice, garnished with toasted sesame seed meal

Appendix 3 COOKING TECHNIQUES AND PREPARATION

The use of certain cooking techniques and natural preservation widens the food choice in winter and early spring particularly in colder countries where the supply of fresh foods may be limited. Although eating vegetables raw maximizes the intake of nutrients, gentle and conservative cooking methods can, in many cases, aid digestion and make certain nutrients more available. This is particularly true for infants and those who cannot chew raw food properly. However, the B group vitamins and vitamin C are all soluble in water and many minerals are leached out during cooking so it is important to use any cooking liquid by adding it to soups or stews. Alternatively, a little finely grated, fresh vegetable or vegetable juice can always be added to soup after it has been removed from the heat in order to ensure that sufficient nutrients are available.

Freezing

The storing of perishable food-stuffs in an insulated cold-storage cabinet is a simple way of preserving food with little loss of nutrients, flavour or appearance.

Many people have found that freezing can be a convenient way of ensuring healthy eating when shortage of time makes cooking every day impossible. Or, when babies are small and only eating tiny amounts, it is often easier to make more puréed fruit or vegetables than you need and freeze the rest in ice cube trays, defrosting one or two cubes as you need them. As the baby gets older you can make salt-free stews or casseroles and freeze meal size portions to use in emergencies. However, it is essential to make sure you always label frozen foods listing ingredients and date of freezing and never refreeze thawed food unless it was raw and you have now cooked it. Most seasonings and flavourings intensify during storage so use less than normal when freezing and semi-liquid foods become thicker so make the mixture more fluid. Beat mixture well if ingredients begin to separate during re-heating. Small quantities freeze better than large amounts and it is advisable to wrap all foods well to prevent a transfer of flavour from one food to another.

Stews, soups and purées are the easiest things to defrost quickly but make sure that if they contain chicken you re-heat them very thoroughly before giving them to your baby or young children, to eliminate any possibility of salmonella poisoning which can occur when improperly cooked chicken is eaten.

Consult a freezer guide book for advice on foods which are unsuitable for freezing, otherwise all recipes given can be frozen if not containing the listed foods.

Boiling

Adding liquid and bringing to boiling point. It removes vitamins and minerals therefore it is important to use the cooking water from vegetables in soups, sauces or as a drink. Few foods are cooked completely at boiling point and most recipes suggest that once boiling point has been reached the heat should be reduced to simmering which is a gentler but still active method. The best way to cook vegetables is in the minimum of water in a suitable sized pot with a tight-fitting lid. True boiling generally involves cooking without a lid if evaporation is required, for example in jam making, or to thicken sauces or reduce the volume of liquid.

Blanching

Plunging vegetables, nuts or meat in to boiling water for 2–3 minutes to prepare them for freezing or for use in salads or as finger foods, or in the case of meat to reduce or remove saltiness or bitterness.

Steaming

Cooking in the vapour or steam of boiling water. Fewer minerals or vitamins are lost by this method in which no water comes in contact with the food. Special steamer pots with perforated bases and collapsable, stainless steel steamers are useful as they fit into different size pots. When steaming in a covered bowl the water in the pot should come half-way up the side of the bowl. Steaming is not a suitable method for cooking meat.

Stewing

Long, slow simmering on top of the oven, it is ideal for cooking stews made from meats, root vegetables and pulses.

Pressure cooking	A method using a strong, hermetically-sealed pot in which food may be cooked quickly at a very high temperature. It can result in overcooking if care is not taken. The use of a heavy pot with a tight-fitting lid, weighted to increase the pressure, is a similar but simpler method.
Braising	Cooking meat and vegetables by lightly browning in fat then simmering in a closed pan with a small amount of liquid. A base of vegetables with barely enough water to cover them, with the meat on top, combines stewing, steaming and pot-roasting methods. The food being braised is basted at intervals with the hot liquid. The resulting stock can be added to a soup or sauce.
Broiling or grilling	A dry method of cooking under, or over, direct heat. It is a way of cooking tender meats and fish which is preferable to frying because it requires little or no added fat or oil.
Roasting or baking	Cooking in the dry heat of the oven, it brings about a number of fascinating chemical changes which produces foods as diverse as meringues, bread, roast meat, pastry, soufflés and custards. These days oven roasting is more common than spit roasting.
Frying	Cooking in fat or oil over a direct heat. Deep-fried foods should not be given to babies or young children as they are very rich and indigestible. Nevertheless they have a place at a later stage and there are a few rules worth learning in order to get the best results. Overheated oil is dangerous as a fire risk and because of the changes that take place in oil at high temperatures it can be harmful to the consumer. If the oil is not hot enough the food being fried will be greasy and difficult to digest. Use top quality, unrefined oil or animal fat heated to below smoking point. Shallow-frying is often used as a preliminary to a moist method of cooking. Shallow-fried onions add flavour but should not be used too frequently for young children.
Stir-frying	Cooking foods quickly in the minimum of oil. The greater availability of the Oriental wok has made this an increasingly popular method of cooking in recent years.
Microwave cooking	Microwave ovens cook the food from the inside out unlike regular cooking which cooks from the outside in. In this method heat is generated in the food but how this affects the delicate molecules of foods cooked in this way and how well equipped the human body is to handle such food remains to be seen. It is recommended here that microwave cookers should be avoided when cooking for children or those with health problems.

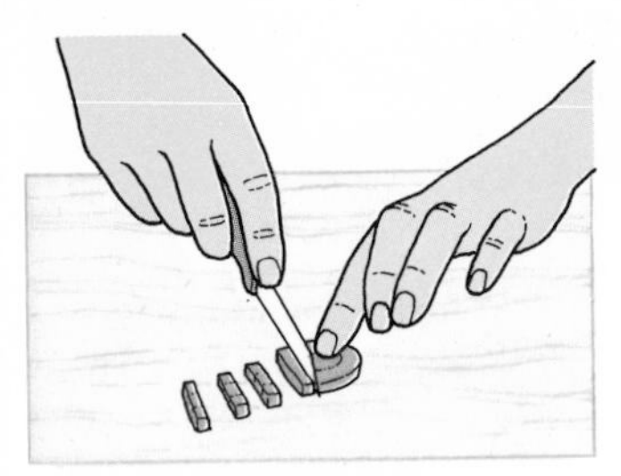

Carrot matchsticks
Slice carrots horizontally
Either reassemble 2–3 slices at a time or take each one individually and cut into thin matchstick strips

Carrot flowers
Cut 4–5 thin wedges out of the full length of the carrot
Slice into rounds of equal thickness

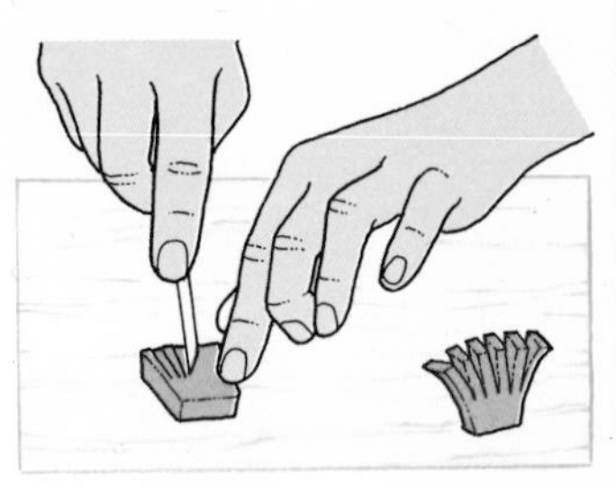

Carrot fans
Cut carrot in half, lengthwise, and trim sides to make even
Cut each half into 3 cm (1¼ in) pieces
Without cutting all the way through, slice each piece into thin strips
When cooked the fan shape opens

Onion dice
Cut onion in half vertically
Lay flat side on hard surface and without cutting all the way through, slice vertically in even strips
Turn onion a semi-circle and repeat, cutting all the way through, to make dice

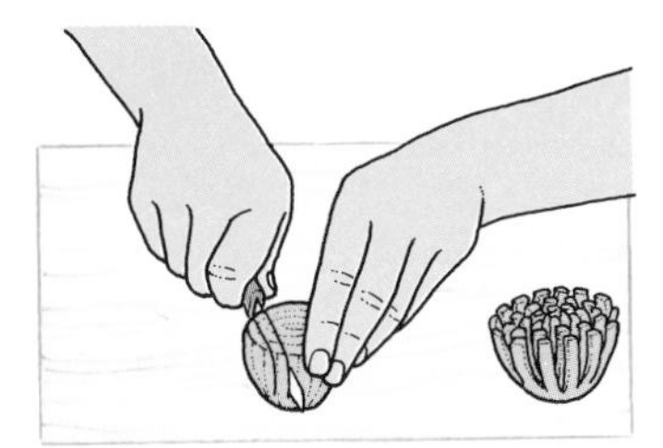

Onion chrysanthemums
Choose small, evenly-sized onions
Stand onion upright on its base
Without cutting right through, slice into thin, vertical strips
Turn onion a semi-circle on its base and cut as above
Soak in cold water to open flower and boil in just enough water to cover

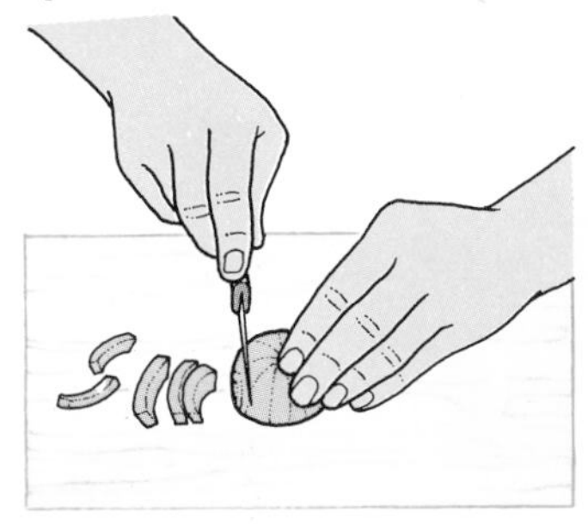

Onion slices
Cut onion in half vertically
Lay flat side down with top of onion at right angles to your body
Cut into even, vertical slices

Debittering

Cut cucumber in half horizontally
Slice off rounded tip and score end of the larger piece with a knife

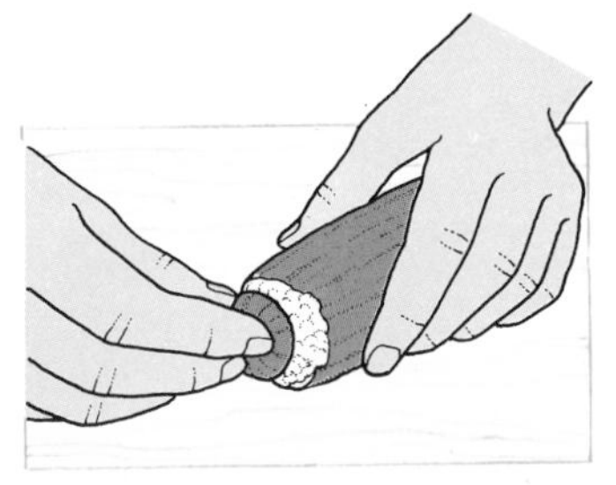

Use cut piece to rub the surface of the scored end in a clockwise direction
Shortly, white foam will appear

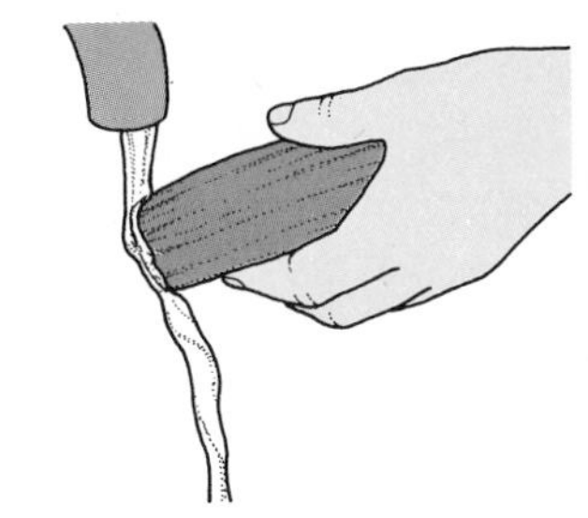

Rub for a further 2 – 3 minutes, then rinse away foam
Repeat with other half of cucumber and use peeled or unpeeled

Standard recipe for pulses (peas, beans and lentils)

(Serves 4–6)

1 CUP (225 g/8 oz) (dry weight)	CUPS OF WATER	COOKING TIME
Split peas	3	30 minutes
Aduki beans	3–4	30–40 minutes
Lentils, split, brown or green	3–4	20–40 minutes
Black-eye beans	3	30 minutes
Butter or broad beans	3	30 minutes
Chickpeas (Do not use under 12 months)	3–4	1½–2 hours

Pre-soak beans for several hours or overnight for larger types. Discard soaking water. Cooking times vary according to type of pot used and pre-soaking. For best results use a heavy pot with a tight-fitting lid. Always boil beans for at least 10 minutes before reducing heat to complete cooking beans until tender.

Add a 15 cm (6 in) piece of kombu seaweed plus the measured water to the pot. The minerals and trace elements released from the kombu make the beans more digestible and flavour-some. Be sure to include this ingredient for your baby from 10 months onward.

Standard recipe for wholegrain cereals

(Serves 4–6)

1 CUP (225 g/8 oz) (dry weight)	CUPS OF WATER	COOKING TIME
Brown rice, short grain	1½–2	40–60 minutes
Soft cooked, baby rice	4–6	1–2 hours
Barley, pot/pearl	2½–3	40–60 minutes
Whole oats	2½–3	40–60 minutes
Whole millet	3	35 minutes
Buckwheat	3	20 minutes
Flaked grains, millet oat, rice, rye, barley	3	10–20 minutes
Buckwheat (soba) noodles	as packet	10–15 minutes

Most grain requires rinsing to remove dust. Combine grain and measured water. The addition of more water and a slightly longer cooking time will give a softer textured grain which is more suitable for sieving in the early stages of weaning. Best results in cooking grain are with the use of a heavy pot with a tight-fitting lid. Bring grain and water to the boil then turn down heat and simmer until all water is absorbed. Do not lift the lid and do not stir during cooking.

Ways to use grains

Barley: added to soups, porridges and casseroles this has a chewier texture than rice.
Whole oats: these have a slightly peppery flavour. A winter favourite is creamy dulse and oat soup. Par-cook and add to barley or oatflakes to make a chewy porridge.
Millet: cooked with vegetables this makes a tasty stew or turned into a mould and sliced when set it can be served with salad.
Buckwheat: available roasted or unroasted this is another winter grain which combines well with pulses and greens.
Buckwheat/soba noodles: use in place of ordinary pasta. Low in wheat or available wheat-free this is a light textured pasta which can be added to soup or served with a bean or mildly flavoured, bolognese-type sauce.

Porridges

Mixed grain, oat and brown rice porridges can be made to suit all tastes and stages. Choose the most appropriate grain and cooking method. Older children and adults find the addition of light tahini, toasted nuts and seeds and soaked dried fruit a deliciously different way to start the day. Good chewing is an essential with such a dish!

Home-made gluten-free baking powder

50 g (2 oz) potassium or sodium bicarbonate
50 g (2 oz) cream of tartar
50 g (2 oz) arrowroot

Sieve all ingredients together several times and store in air-tight jar. Use as regular brands.
Many commercial brands of baking powder contain wheat and other additives so it is useful to be able to make your own.

NB In all recipes the ingredients and serving amounts are approximate.
The amount of fluid given in any recipe will vary according to the type of flour used.
All recipes can be varied to suit tastes and needs by substituting similar ingredients – weight for weight. For example, soya or goat's milk for cow's milk; barley malt or molasses for syrup.

USEFUL ADDRESSES

Foresight
c/o Mrs P. Barnes
The Old Vicarage
Church Lane
Witley
Godalming
Surrey GU8 5PN
Telephone (Wormley) 042879-4500

The association for the promotion of pre-conceptual care

The Hahnemann Society
Humane Education Centre
Avenue Lodge
Bounds Green Road
London N22 4EU

Annual subscription UK £5, overseas £6 includes quarterly magazine *Homoeopathy Today*

Homoeopathic Medicine Suppliers
A. Nelson & Co. Ltd.
73 Duke Street
London W1
Telephone 01-629 3118

Mail order
5 Endeavour Way
Wimbledon
London SE19 9UH
Telephone 01-946-8527

Henry Doubleday Research Association
c/o Lawrence D. Hills
Convent Lane
Bocking
Braintree
Essex

Send sae for expert advice on organic gardening

Hyperactive Children's Support Group
c/o S. Bunday
59 Meadowside
Angmering
West Sussex BN16 4BW

La Leche League of Great Britain
P.O. Box BM 3424
London WC1V 6XX
Telephone 01-404-5011

National Childbirth Trust
9 Queensborough Terrace
London W2
Telephone 01-229-9319

National Eczema Society
26 Jessica Road
London SW18
Telephone 01-874-1963

The Vegan Society
47 Highlands Road
Leatherhead
Surrey

The Vegetarian Society
Parkdale
Durham Road
Altrincham
Cheshire WA14 4QG
Telephone 061-928-0793

Nursing Mothers Association of Australia
National headquarters
357 Burwood Road
Hawthorn
Victoria 3122
Telephone 03-818-8031

La Leche League of New Zealand Inc.
P.O. Box 2307
Christchurch
New Zealand
Telephone 03-793-938

The New Zealand Vegetarian Society
P.O. Box 454
Auckland 1
New Zealand

La Leche League in Canada
Box 70
Williamsburg
Ontario KOC 2HO
Telephone 613-535-2536

Toronto Vegetarian Society
Robert Neilly
P.O. Box 7137
Station A
Toronto M5W 1XB

The Entropy Institute
Dr Ross Hume Hall
Box 984
Station A
Hamilton
Ontario L89 3RI

FURTHER READING

Cook Yourself a Favour
Drs S. and R. Gibson and L. Templeton SRD
Johnston Green Publishers Ltd 1983

Laurel's Kitchen
Robertson, Flinders and Godfrey
Routledge and Kegan Paul 1979

Cooking with Care and Purpose
Michel Absehra
Swan House Publishers 1978

Nutrition and Health
Sir Robert McCarrison
McCarrison Press 1982

The Book of Whole Meals
A. Colbin
Autumn Press 1981

100% Gluten Free Bake Book
Cantassium Jubilee
Rita Greer
The Cantassium Company 1980

Breast is Best
Drs Andrew and Penny Stanway
Pan 1978

The Breastfeeding Book
Máire Messenger
Century Publishing Company 1982

Food Combining for Health
Doris Grant and Jean Joyce
Thorsons 1984

Having a Baby Easily
Margaret Brady
Thorsons 1981

Good Food Gluten Free
H. C. Hills
Roberts Publications 1976

Food for Thought
A new look at food and behaviour
Drs Saul and Jo Anne Miller
Prentice Hall Inc 1979

Cooking the New Diabetic Way
Available from:
The British Diabetic Association,
10 Queen Anne Street, London W1

Homoeopathy for the Family
Available from:
The Homoeopathic Development Foundation,
Suite 1, 19A Cavendish Square,
London W1M 9AD

Homoeopathy for Mother and Infant
and *First Aid Homoeopathy*
Available from:
The British Homoeopathic Association,
27a Devonshire St London W1N 1RJ

What Every Mum and Dad Should Know About British Standards
Available from:
The British Standard Institute,
2 Park Street, London W1A 2EBS
55p (P&P)

ACKNOWLEDGEMENTS

Author's Acknowledgements

Grateful thanks of appreciation are due to many people who, over the past years, have contributed to my interest in and understanding of nutrition. In this particular instance I should like to thank all those who have contributed to this book, professionally and intuitively, especially the editors Nicky Foy, Pippa Rubinstein, Clare Meek and Esther Eisenthal; Art Director, Debbie MacKinnon; Art Editor, Sandra Schneider; Louise Tucker, Dr Franklin and Sue Lupson; and finally love and thanks to my parents, who have been a constant source of good sense and humour.

Publishers acknowledgements

The publishers, the photographer and the author would like to thank the following for allowing us to photograph them for this book: Susie and Taig Griffin, Sally-Ginger Brockbank, Emma, Nicholas and Linda Kay, Nellie Green, Jill, Claudio and Isobel Newsome, Caroline, Mick and Roxanne Smee, Jolyon Rubinstein, Sam Gordon, Deborah and Raphael Schneebeli, Phoebe Foy Phillips, Oakley Walters, Christopher Blackburn, Debbie, Mike and Polly Staniford, Marian, Layla and Debbie Ghorbannefad, Julie and Tom Lascelles, Karen Shein.

INDEX

Editor: Nicky Foy
Art editor: Sandra Schneider
Series editor: Pippa Rubinstein

Art director: Debbie MacKinnon

Illustrations by Coral Mula, Brenda Armitt
and Lorna Turpin
Retouching by Nick Oxtoby
Photographic prints by John Marlow
Artwork by Radius

Filmset by D. P. Media Limited
Hitchin, Hertfordshire